OVERTHINKING

A Useful Guide to Free your Mind from Negative Thoughts, Provide New Positive Energy to Your Life and Find the Way to Stop Worrying and End Anxiety, take action and Be Yourself

JEFFREY MIND

Copyright 2019 by Jeffrey Mind - All rights reserved.

This eBook is provided with the sole purpose of providing relevant information on a specific topic for which every reasonable effort has been made to ensure that it is both accurate and reasonable. Nevertheless, by purchasing this eBook, you consent to the fact that the author, as well as the publisher, are in no way experts on the topics contained herein, regardless of any claims as such that may be made within. As such, any suggestions or recommendations that are made within are done so purely for entertainment value. It is recommended that you always consult a professional prior to undertaking any of the advice or techniques discussed within.

This is a legally binding declaration that is considered both valid and fair by both the Committee of Publishers Association and the American Bar Association and should be considered as legally binding within the United States.

The reproduction, transmission, and duplication of any of the content found herein, including any specific or extended information, will be done as an illegal act regardless of the end form the information ultimately takes. This includes copied versions of the work, both physical, digital, and audio unless the express consent of the Publisher is provided beforehand. Any additional rights reserved.

Furthermore, the information that can be found within the pages described forthwith shall be considered both accurate and truthful when it comes to the recounting of facts. As such, any use, correct or incorrect, of the provided information will render the Publisher free of responsibility as to the actions taken outside of their direct purview. Regardless, there are zero scenarios where the original author or the Publisher can be deemed liable in any fashion for any damages or hardships that may result from any of the information discussed herein.

Additionally, the information in the following pages is intended only for informational purposes and should thus be thought of as universal. As befitting its nature, it is presented without assurance regarding its prolonged validity or interim quality. Trademarks that are mentioned are done without written consent and can in no way be considered an endorsement from the trademark holder.

Table of Contents

Conclusion

Introduction

The following chapters will discuss Overthinking, which as its name suggests, thinking too much and long about the anxiety-inducing occurrence, usually but not always a negative experience of some kind (e.g., past mistake, current concern, or future outcome). Do you find it hard to shut down your racing mind? Do you feel fatigued and troubled because of your thoughts? If so, you are likely an acute overthinker. Today, overthinking is an international epidemic, since we live in difficult and demanding times that require so much mental capacity from us to function and succeed in. Adult responsibilities, money, mental trauma, and other problems leave our minds active 24/7. After thorough research, psychology professor Susan Nolen-Hoeksema from the University of Michigan found that young and middle-aged adults are especially prone to overthinking with 73% of 25-35-year-olds identified as overthinkers. Unsurprisingly, more women (57%) than men (43%) identify themselves as overthinkers; men are more likely to distract or detach themselves from their thoughts and feelings. So, if you have trouble controlling your thoughts and feel weighed down by them, this book will provide you an overview and guide to stop overthinking and recognize the subtle signs of overthinking. Now that you know what overthinking is, it is important to emphasize that overthinking is not inherently negative or wrong. Everyone automatically overthinks from time to time due to the hectic and demanding nature of modern life (e.g., Mortgage, career expectations, children, finances, etc.). With that being said, there comes the point when everything, especially future decisions can lead to unknown anxiety and negative outcomes; at which point, doing nothing is preferable to taking a risk and facing the unknown consequences of your decisions. At this point, overthinking becomes a problem.

The next question is how to assess and solve the unconscious problem of overthinking. Firstly, it is important to understand what causes overthinking. Beyond mental issues such as depression and anxiety, other contributing factors include experiencing childhood abuse, neglect, a traumatic event, being a perfectionist, having a genetic predisposition, and introversion. Using the following checklist, you can determine if you meet the threshold for overthinking or not: the need for perfectionism, insomnia, burnout, requiring others feedback on unimportant matters, irritability, occasional hypochondriasis, consistent sadness/negative thinking, and a believed lack of control over parts of life.

After realizing that you suffer from overthinking, you've taken the first step towards resolving the problem. The next steps are to recognize cognitive biases, identify which ones apply most to you, be conscious of your thought processes all through the day, challenge your knee-jerk thoughts and replace your cognitive biases with reality. If necessary, consider professional psychiatric help to overcome mental health issues, especially if you've suffered from childhood abuse.

In order to keep overthinking at bay and find peace of mind, consider adopting a stoic approach to life, break negative thought habits, engage in meditation and relaxation techniques to calm the mind, and sleep well. Also, be sure to cultivate positive energies and thinking into your life to prevent yourself from overthinking. This is best accomplished through loving yourself by learning the true meaning of this cliché phrase and how it differs from narcissism; with self-love being about valuing and taking regard for your own happiness and well-being and narcissism defined by its excessive vanity need for admiration from others to cover up one's own insecurities and low-self-esteem about themselves. Lastly, it is vital to always have in mind that you can conquer overthinking and to accept yourself, in spite of all your flaws because you are not the sum of all your mistakes or failures. There are plenty of books on this subject on the market, thanks again for choosing this one! Every effort was made to ensure it is full of as much useful information as possible, and please enjoy it!

Jeffrey Mind

Chapter 1

Overthinking

Overthinking. It's the sleepless nights caused by past regrets that continue to haunt your mind. It's worrying about the potential future as you brood over negative experiences in the past. It's every paralyzing fear. It's always thinking that you'll fail no matter what, whether it be failing a class, at a job, or in relationships. There are often unrealistic expectations for success underlying overthinking, which must be met, and it takes an exhausting toll on you. It is both physically and emotionally exhausting because the brain that never slows or shuts down. Overthinking is the pause between texts as you wonder how they interpreted what you said. It's typing out and deleting a text, only to send another one because you are not comfortable with what you've written. It's the never-ending need for answers and responses to keep your mind satisfied.

Overthinking is the critical voice that brings you down because it doubts everybody and everything around you, especially yourself, bringing up your mistakes and decisions. When you overthink things, you never just go with your gut feeling. It's helplessly going down the self-destructive path your mind leads you down. It is like an uncontrolled wildfire that destroys all opposition in its path. Overthinking feels like you're always sitting tight for something, yet you don't really know what it is: for something to change, somebody to become distraught or a situation to end badly due to your own fault. Overthinking makes you feel unnecessarily sorry because you're upset for questioning and thinking the worst of people. It causes you to always imagine the worst-case scenario. Overthinking causes you to become excessively wary of everything. It's the dread of relationships since you require so much from a partner that you wonder if you would be better off alone. Because is it even possible to explain to a partner that it isn't you, I doubt or distrust, my mind is causing me to be so wary? How do you explain to a potential partner that you need to hear constant reassurance regarding your relationship or yourself? It's never certain whether someone truly likes you or is just tolerating you for the time being. As a result, you require consolation for each uncertainty. It always requires someone to be completely truthful and clarify any uncertainties about everything. Even if this might seem a bit too much, it is the only way to keep the painful assumptions caused by overthinking at bay. It believes situations that are genuine in your mind despite the fact that it's completely out there to a normal individual. Overthinking is caring too much about someone else's trivial opinion or an ignored text that shouldn't affect you, but in actuality, you are questioning what I have done wrong? And what can I do to fix it?

As you can see, overthinking is more than simply thinking too much about something, usually a negative experience such as past or current issues (ex. Finances, marriage, children, mistakes, regrets, etc.), events or conversations which grabs and holds your attention. Whether it be internally scolding themselves for a mistake they made yesterday or worrying over their performance tomorrow: an overthinker is characterized by these troubling thoughts—and their inability to stop thinking, which leaves them in a perpetual state of misery. Everybody overthinks from time to time, whether it be their decisions, present concerns, or behavior. This is predominantly true in this modern age, where the internet has resulted in information overload through social media and self-help information providing ample sources of anxiety and self-doubt. Modern life has also become overwhelmingly hectic and demanding with stressors arising from multiple sources: career, family, finances, mortgage, marriage, etc. Overthinking is quite literally an automatic habit that we have little conscious control of. Our brains are literally wired for overthinking with all our memories, thoughts, and emotions all interconnected into spiderweb networks of connections, which we refer back to in times of thought. However, although this ability made us more effective thinkers due to our ability to avoid painful outcomes (criticism, rejection, failure, illness, etc.) through our previous experiences, it can also paralyze our decision making.

Anxiety, worry, and self-doubt are feelings that are commonly experienced together by overthinkers as well and only exacerbates the problem. Anxiety is an emotion defined by an unpleasant and unrestful feeling, usually expressed as nervous behaviors such as physical distress, pacing back and forth, and deep reflection. It's a personal feeling of panic-stricken fear and apprehension at an expected future event, such as the feeling of your own impending demise. Anxiety and overthinking usually go together hand in hand. One of the most common signs of an anxiety disorder is a disposition towards overthinking. The brain that is constantly on-edge is hyperaware, continuously on guard for anything it seems to be unsafe or troubling. An overthinker would see issues even when there aren't any. Why? Because anxiety causes one to overthink everything in many different ways, and the result of this overthinking doesn't provide any closure or reassurance to your worries. Worry is strongly connected to anxiety and refers broadly to the continual and frantic images, feelings, and negative actions undergone by the mind to avoid or solve potential problems and their outcomes as part of an automatic risk analysis. For example, continually and frantically imagining your exam tomorrow and how you will act to succeed on it because you don't want to fail. However, there is always the looming feeling of actually failing or doing poorly on your exam, which results in feelings of distress and dread that grips you and won't let go while self-doubt is usually being unconfident or uncertain regarding one's own abilities, success, or actions. It is a pervasive feeling of failure and regret behind any new and bold pursuit you undertake because you feel like you aren't experienced or skilled enough to accomplish your goal. As you can see, the co-morbid conditions of overthinking: anxiety, worry, and self-doubt are all linked to the body's reaction to stress, which is a physical, mental, or emotional agent that responds to bodily or mental strain. It is the body's way of responding to any imminent threat or demand by switching into a rapid automated procedure best known as the "fight-or-flight response."

The fight-or-flight response is how the body protects you. It is intended to help you stay focused, energized, and aware in a potentially life-threatening situation to have the best survival chances. This can be through providing you additional strength to defend yourself, or driving you are to slam the breaks to avoid a car accident. Stress also gives you the capability to tackle obstacles. It's what keeps you motivated during exam studying time when you'd rather be slacking off, sharpens your concentration during an exam, and drives you to accomplish everything on your agenda. In this case, stress is a normal part of life that everyone experiences to give them the push to get through their day. But at some point, you can be under too much stress, and that's when it's no longer beneficial because it begins to cause major damage to your physical and mental health and well-being. In our modern lives, there are more causes of overwhelming stress than ever before, in the form of career expectations, children, finances, marriage, and relationships. This results in us being in a constant state of stress, which we can't unwind from because they are present everywhere, leaving us automatically overthinking in an attempt to find a solution or plan to solve our troubles amidst an ocean of anxiety, self-doubt, and possibilities. To a degree, this is a good thing because it allows us to reflect upon our problems and weigh potential solutions; in which case, overthinking is closer in nature to problem-solving or planning. We all require some degree of planning and thinking in our lives. However, the stressors of hectic and competitive modern life have given way to more reasons for sleepless nights spent excessively overthinking than ever before, with demands (e.g., career expectations, mortgage, finances, family, marriage, etc.) affecting every aspect of your life. This is especially true when it comes to taking decisive action, of which there are numerous potentially bad outcomes that anxiously immobilizes your decision-making. In this case, overthinking prevents us from taking decisive action when we need to rather than serving its original role in finding the best course of action. Social media and the internet only serve to exacerbate this problem by providing an over-idealized version of life and information overload in the form of self-help and improvement guides. The result is a perfect image or standard that we feel obligated to meet in order to fit in, but of which we always fall short of no matter what, resulting in endless anxiety, worry, and self-doubt.

While these are all key aspects of our lives that we all hope to be successful in, it is ultimately out of our control more times than not. We can't control our partners, bosses, children, markets, or economy, which determines the outcome of our lives. Regardless, they become the source of many of our sleepless nights spend overthinking and worrying as a result. It can start off as a random negative thought (Why did I make a mistake at work today?) which moves on towards anxiously obsessing over every small detail (circumstances, the order of events, emotional impact, what-ifs, effects, or consequences) of the experience in question rather than solving the actual underlying problem. At this point, it is key to point out that overthinking is often a symptom of a root mental problem such as depression, trauma, PTSD, agoraphobia, or an anxiety disorder characterized by constant and excessive stress, worrying, and dwelling on the past. There is also an element of self-doubt in overthinking as well due to over-analysis causing one to become unconfident of one's own capabilities and logic. Left unchecked, overthinking will cause you to become consumed by anguish, and unrealistic panic from everything that has gone or could go wrong, exacerbated by a mental problem. If you think rather than taking decisive action and accomplishing things, you are overthinking. If you analyze, reflect, and think about the same thoughts repeatedly rather than taking action, you are overthinking. This mental habit paralyzes you from taking action in your life. It also drains your energy, takes away your decision-making capability, and throws you into a never-ending loop of thinking the exact same thing. This cyclical thinking uses up all your time and energy and prevents you from making decisions, trying new things, and progressing in life. It's like a hamster running on its wheel, going around and round but remaining in the same place. As a result, overthinkers have an increased likelihood of worry, anxiety, and inner anguish compared to non-overthinkers.

Now that you know the processes, factors, and effects of overthinking, two dangerous thought patterns—ruminating and worrying eventually emerge in overthinking. Ruminating is carefully and obsessively going over a thought or problem repeatedly without ever finishing it. Whether it be repeating an old argument, comment, or mistake in your mind like a broken record, your mind just cannot seem to let it go no matter. Ruminating is heavily connected with depression due to the fact that the mental condition causes you to continually remember the worst aspects of yourself. Examples include:

I shouldn't have spoken up at yesterday's meeting. Everybody looked at me like I'm such an idiot.

I wish I had dropped out of university. I would've been so much further ahead in life by now if I had.

My parents said that I was worthless and couldn't amount to anything. I guess they were right.

You can see the self-defeating aspect of ruminating, one of the most dangerous aspects of overthinking because it paralyzes you from taking action. What's the point, if you'll just going to fail, no matter how hard you try or its already too late to turn around from a previous bad decision? As you can already tell, rumination is a reflection of how one views themselves and is thus deeply rooted in self-esteem and image. Negative self-esteem and image have several causes (media, belief systems, bullying), but the most common reason is your parents or guardians. Parents do have the largest impact on their children growing up after all. If they were abusive, neglectful, uninvolved towards you growing up, it'd result in lower self-esteem or image growing up. This is further possibly exacerbated if you have a history of academic, athletic, or social underperformance during your formative years and are compared to your higher-performing peers constantly. Without any obvious talents to make you think otherwise, it is easy to feel like you're a nobody in society compared to everyone else. As you already know, worry is your brain anticipating potential problems and outcomes in an effort to avoid them, but they tend to be negative - usually disastrous future predictions:

I'm going to fail the test tomorrow. I'll totally blank out, forget everything, and end up failing out of school.

I'll never get my driver's license. It is not important how hard I try or what I do. It's never going to happen.

I'll never get my dream job. There is always going to be someone better than me. I should just play it safe and work a stable and well-paying career I hate.

As you can see, ruminating and worry are closely related to each other; both cause one to think negatively, whatever it be about oneself or a situation. However, rumination and worry are only states of mind and can be resolved. This will be covered in a future cover. Ultimately, overthinking is defined by its two self-destructive patterns – worrying and ruminating, but it still serves an important role in problem-solving in our lives when engaged into an extent.

Chapter 2

Recognizing a Problem

"The first phase in resolving a problem is to acknowledge that it exists"-Zig Ziglar-as mentioned before, it is totally ordinary to overthink one step; everyone is at moments susceptible to it. Working with ruminating can also be helpful instruments to solve your problems. Worry makes you think the worst situation, like failure to perform a test and do everything you can to prevent it. During rumor, you remember past errors and other adverse times so that you do not repeat them again. However, overthinking becomes an issue when your whole life is consumed with fear and paralyzed by actions. These are nine prevalent indications of concern and rumor about your existence and the way to fix it.

1. Constant insomnia

Falling asleep is a task for all rebellious thinkers. Thinking overwhelms your capacity to slow your thinking as you slowly paralyze your decision-making. Always your mind is active and sleepy; all your concerns and regret plague your mind, and your own mental hell cannot leave you. You can't escape. All of this is combined to make the ideal insomnia recipe.

Try relaxing before heading to sleep, for example, meditation, Yoga, light training, artistic workouts, or even speaking with family and friends to help relieve your insomnia. Do something that gets your ideas off while offering your creativity and your feelings in particular.

2. Fear for the future

You spend too much time in your mind when you have a fear of the future. Nolen-Hoeksema discovered in her studies that such anxiety leads to the use of alcohol and medicines by rethinkers to deal with potential anxieties.

You should be a meditation practice or any other activity that promotes awareness and the present to deal with this symptom of overthinking. An additional concept is to offer yourself an "outlet" to overthink. Please take 15 to 30 minutes a day to let all of your concerns go by writing or speaking with a friend. This way, you can proceed with your day without your concerns being burdened.

3. Overviewing everything

The root issue of all overthinkers is that everything in their life must be controlled. They have to decide their own future, but it is very anxious because they can't foresee it. They do not like to do anything they cannot regulate completely, and they are immensely frightened of the unknown, which leads them to sit and think about every option rather than committing themselves to action. In reality, a UC Santa Barbara research found that overthrowing effectively produced worse decisions and judgments than stronger ones in general. After all, it seems your intestine is truly legitimate.

In order to resolve this, attempt to return into the current by breathing deeply and concentrating your thoughts on relaxing stuff when you rethink yourself. Try to look at the uselessness of these ideas at current and prevent them, as you will discover that these ideas only cause pressure.

4. Excessive fear of failure

The overthinkers must all be perfectionists. They cannot experience failure and make every effort to prevent it. However, only by doing nothing can this happen. The fear of death paralyzes the overthinker, so they prefer to do anything to ensure they don't succeed rather than risk failure.

Recall that your previous errors and failures are not defined by you if this defines you correctly. Recall that the inability to make strides in life is necessary. Failure can help you learn, develop, and enhance.

5. Continually second-guessing yourself

A second guess continuously because they seek defectiveness, overthinking people constantly evaluate, evaluate, and evaluate all situations therein three times. You don't want to make the right choice, so it takes a long time to make a choice because you don't think of yourself. They're out of touch with their instinct, so it makes every choice logical, and that doesn't work out always. You are clearly a reverse thinker if you have a brain so foggy and hindered that you cannot make a definite decision. Learn to go instinct and intestine. If it happens incorrect, you've at least taught and acquired more life-experience.

6. Common Headaches

You probably believe too much if you have headaches frequently. Headaches say our bodies we need a break; this is also true for our heads. Moreover, if you maintain an eye on your ideas, you will discover you imagine the same stuff again and again. Workers tend to have adverse thought processes, so instead, change over gradually to favorable ideas to combat this. Concentrate on your breathing and attention, and in no moment will you get lost with headaches.

7. Muscle and joint pain

After you become a component of your brain, and until it is administered, you can become physically active as a fantasy muscle and joint pain without any medical cause. Although it begins to overthrow your head, it will eventually cause exhaustion and fatigue in the areas of your body. To prevent this, work out and frequently stretch before heading to bed. This will assist you to get your mind and body healthy. The mind and body are so interrelated that a decrease in one's situation also affects the other.

8. Constant Fatigue

Constantly weary fatigue is indicative of an issue that must be resolved. Our bodies need us to take care that they send them rather than keep going our day and overlook their significant posts. Although fatigue is usually triggered by overwork, it can also carry you off by overthinking. It makes sense if you stop and believe about it; you'll push your brain to its border by ultimately overthrowing and burning it. Without necessarily getting completely exhausted, the mind cannot operate 24/7 at maximum rates. This is caused in our contemporary life by its hectic and-stopping speed, which means that in too little time over-analysis, we have to do much. We don't have the free time to concentrate on our own wellness in our busy schedules. In the past, this was not true when we lived with nature and concentrated only on our own life; chasing, collecting, and farming enough that we were able to achieve a fairly lying pace not subject to rigid timetables or time limits. Take mental wellness days to concentrate on your mind and body's wants to cope with your tiredness.

9. Not living in the moment

If you can no longer live and enjoy life as it happens, this is a consequence of overthrowing. Overthink leads you to lose track and experience of the globe. It keeps you away from the rest because you're always caught in your own head. Make sure you open your mind and heart to the globe and not become stuck in adverse thought processes. Concentrate on thinking in a positive fashion and disregard adverse ideas. For those who live in the moment rather than in heads, the world offers countless possibilities for personal connections and experiences. Connections with others also help to calm these adverse aspects. When we establish private contacts with others, our adverse ideas can be kept silent by our attendant. Our friendships also enable us to turn our attention back and adverse ideas towards others. Learn to hear, connect with, and learn more about others. Chronic rethinking is an issue that can be resolved by building powerful groups that allow us to help one another and also gives us a chance to learn from each other.

As you can see in these nine indications, overthinking is not only an issue that binds up your thinking and decision making and causes decreases, but also positively impacts your mental and physical health. This leads to an enhanced danger of emotional disorders, such as depression and fear. Unchecked, overthinking, your work quality, your relationship, your body, and your mind will be destroyed. You now understand the indications of rethinking being turned into an issue, and now you can hear about its effects, fear, fear, and rumination. It is not only irritating to overthink stuff; it can impact your health seriously. Research shows that your imperfections, mistakes, and troubles are ruminating, raises your likelihood of mental health issues, including depression and anxiety. And as your mind's health worsens, you are ruminated more often, leading in a hard to break the self-destructive cycle. Studies also reveal that rethinking creates severe mental pain, which patients are treated with unsanitary treatments, including tobacco, alcohol, medicines, or foods. Sleeplessness has also been connected with rethinking with research confirming this; rumination and concern have shown less sleeping hours and less performance. Unhealthy practices, bad sleep and overthinking mental circumstances lead to severe health issues (e.g., cancer, cardiac diseases, heart disease, pancreatitis, and an aggregates reduction of life). It is essential to know what is really going on in your mind when you are overwhelmed before moving into the specifics of the effects of overthinking and associated mental disorders (e.g., stress, concern, anxiety, and depression), i.e., an incident, an individual, a previous occurrence, or an issue

- You just continue to think, you cannot shake a sensation, but you do not think of a remedy, you are crucial, and you act.
- Whenever a bad thing happens, your mind automatically turns to the most diaspora scenarios and asks, "what if? "And" why?".

- You sometimes run into adverse models of thought.

- You are excessively worried about mistakes or issues and worries and may contribute to adverse results.

- You are concerned about your everyday experience and personal relationships or over-analyze them.

- You extend every phrase, concept, and condition to a greater extent than sensitive and realistic ratios and pick up stuff that is not there at first.

With anxiety, they race through our hearts not only, but also through our hearts, 24/7. Like a hamster hooked into an infinite fall in energy beverage, it always goes but never runs. At the same time, we are tired and energized by fear and rethink. One outcome of anxiety overthink is that you feel physically and mentally ill. The same worrying ideas run through our heads 24/7, irrespective of what we feel.

In addition, an additional hazardous side impact of fear is that we finally begin to think of our own ideas. After all, if we think enough of its validity, then it's genuine. Is this not? Is it not? No. No. That's an anxiety side-effect. Anxiety creates reversal, but under no conditions can worried ideas be trusted. The unhealthy impacts of unnecessary anxiety will give the affected a lifespan of more disease. Below is a list of side effects of dangerous anxiety.

The patient residing with a generalized anxiety disease without treatment or controls may suffer several signs and implications because anxiety can adversely influence every aspect of everyday lives.

- Inability to meet home, work, and college duties
- Sleeping issues
- Family and marriage issues
- Difficulty in carrying out regular operations
- Inability to concentrate
- Inability to normalize socialization with others
- Agoraphobia
- Helplessness with your situation
- Diminished self-esteem from the emotions of hopelessness
- loss of self-drive

These troubling ideas lead to continuous adverse stimuli in your body to cope with the effects of your stressful state. The human nervous system cannot tell the distinction between mental and physical threats, as you see. If a contention with a buddy, a work date, or a high-end bill pile is compressed and subdued, your body can react the same as in the case of a true life-or-death case... Furthermore, the easier it is to start up and to overcome the stress issue, the longer you activate your contingency or flight scheme. You are constantly under heavy stress in the challenging and modern world complete of innumerable strains. This can lead to serious health issues. Almost everybody unit is affected by acute pressure. It can intimidate your immune system, interrupt your digestive and reproductive processes, boost the danger of heart attacks and accidents. It can even redirect your brain neural networks, which makes you at increased danger for fear, depression, and other issues in your mental health.

Stress-related or aggravating health issues include:

1. Anxiety and Depression
2. Agony
3. Lack of sleep
4. Self-immune illnesses
5. Problems with digestion
6. Problems with the skin like eczema
7. Heart illness
8. Issues of Weight
9. Reproductive problems
10. Thought and mental problems

The most hazardous element of stress is how it can surprise you completely. Thinking and memory issues. You don't believe that you'll be influenced. You start to feel familiar, almost like your buddies. But even when you pay a high cost, you do not understand how much stress affects you. This is the motivation why it is vital to comprehend the prevalent hazard indications and stress meltdown symptoms.

The issue is caused by every day too much worry and anxiety in fighting or flying. The combat or flight reaction leads to stress hormones (signal molecules) like cortisol sending into the bloodstream in the sympathetic system of the body. These hormones can improve blood sugar concentrations and body oil triglyceride (Blood fats). The hormones also produce a physical effect like:

- Dry mouth
- Increased Heartbeats
- Focus lessness
- Irritability
- Muscle dullness
- muscle stress
- Feeling sickly
- Fast breathing
- Short breaths
- Sweating
- Shaking and Muscle Spasms

If additional oxygen in the body does not burn for physical activity. Also, although these side effects are a response to pressure, it is essential to remember that stress is merely the trigger. It varies on how you handle stress, whether you get tired or not. Your immune, heart, and blood vessels, as well as how certain glans discharge hormones in your body, are physically stress related. The role of these hormones is to help manage body activities, such as brain and nerve pulses. All these schemes are linked and are affected by your mental condition and coping style. You don't feel tired of stress. Rather, it is the effect on these different interconnected structures which can produce a physical disease that is too worrying and anxious. Some stuff you can do, like good lifestyle modifications to make your pressure reaction more viable and sensitive.

Finally, depression is frequently linked to its trigger: fear, concern, and overthrow, and it is renowned for various severe physical and mental health issues, including:

- feeling sad and empty
- insomnia
- absorption of death and self-injury (risk of suicide)
- problem memory and decision-making
- needlessness of mind

- the danger of a heart attack
- the danger of exhaustion
- risk of suicide.

Anticipation

Preview is the beginning trap too early. It's true we may not have sufficient time to complete if we begin too early. But penalties also apply to start too early. We are responsible for overwork, prework, and work in vain when we anticipate.

If we act now, then we overwork if the same result can be achieved more easily later. Here is a well-constructed instance of the complexity of this trap. We write two answers, one for each option, in expectation of a letter of recognition or refusal. If we had waited for the letter to be received, we had only to do half the work, and the result was the same. We overworked, therefore. In this situation, the overwork is so clear that it would only be carried out by the most heavily caught. However, many of us would not be able to reflect on every response from time to time. Half of these thinking is meant to be unnecessary.

Naturally, if we wait, the findings are not always the same. There may be insufficient time to complete the task well later. Now, if a subsequent beginning would jeopardize the result, it is not a trick to behave. But much of what we do every day can be accomplished at other times as well. If we don't have a weekend postal service, we can just mail a letter on Monday afternoon or on Sunday. Exactly the same outcomes are achieved. The best moment to behave in this situation is when this invariant outcome can be achieved at the lowest price at the moment, power, and money.

If the costs are the same over a period, then it will be as good for every other period to get the job done. But sometimes are often more appropriate than others for intervention. For instance, if we expect to pass a mailbox on Monday, on the way to work, a special trip to the mailbox on Sundays would be anticipated. From the beginning, there is nothing that could compensate for the additional job. Likewise, there would usually not be any benefit if the answer—or even an answer—was to be written before it was received instead of afterward. We should, therefore, wait for the work to be simplified.

This assessment is not valuable for the job of its own accord. When we send our e-mail on Sunday because we want to go on a lovely day, we don't waste our time, even though we leave again the same place on Monday evening. This little excuse to go out is a pleasure for us. It's never a trap to do what we like.

In general, the job is simplified over the course of time. Delay allows the arrival of fresh data that could save us difficulty. A stronger strategy can come into perspective before we commit to a certain strategy. Before we butt our heads against them, dead ends may be disclosed. We could obtain a fresh instrument to make the job easier. In particular, the amount of contingencies that need to be taken into consideration is constantly diminished as families with opportunities coalesce into individual truths. We only have one true letter in place of two feasible letters to reply to. There are only two choices to choose from when we complete primary education rather than ten professional alternatives that are consistent with what we learn about our concerns and skills when we complete the 6th grade. Over the moment, the work simplifies itself.

This doesn't imply we should leave it all until the last minute. We can't delay our plans until departure if we want to move to the Orient. Too much can be achieved merely. Our passports, visas, vaccines, and controls on tourists must be obtained; we must warn our employers to help the cat find temporary homes. It is true that subsequently, we can find easier methods to perform some of these duties. However, we have no chance to do anything unless we take this danger. But if a job is postponed without jeopardizing the opportunity of completing it promptly, it should be postponed. Because our activities are based on the recent and finest data, we are losing nothing.

Predictive overworking is strongly associated with the amplification phenomenon. The distinction is that certain occurrences are organized on a temporal basis.

If we overwork because of expectations, we can do the same work with less effort if we are waiting for a more favorable time. Right now, the same work can be performed easier when we amplify.

Anticipation may result in prework if there is a possibility that the evolving conditions will reverse our job. Once we have prepared both admission and dismissal responses early, there will be an unforeseen third alternative: an application for more data. Now we didn't just work harder than we needed. Our job has come to nothing in this situation. From scratch, we must start again. We could have watched TV as well. What we did is just an unnecessary preliminary to the actual task. It was precautionary.

Certainly, by altering conditions, we can never completely prevent the reversal of our job. We are conducting thorough research into the comparative advantages of Florida and Arizona as retirement homes, and their personality change so dramatically within a couple of years that all of our calculations become outdated. Regardless of how late we behave, at the last minute, the Universe can still take the carpet from our feet. However, without any prospect of compensation, it is useless to raise this danger. We must eventually behave or endure excessive delay punishment. However, it should be delayed as soon as the job can be delayed without penalties. Because by allowing the world to develop its scheme more before we behave, we reduce the likelihood of our job being lost.

In existential anticipation, there is a unique and extreme form of pre-working.

In judging the nature and quality of existence in its entirety, we fall into this trap. If we want life sufficiently happy or meaningful to satisfy the standards, we set for it, it is impossible to fulfill our objective or to fail it certainly until life itself is ended. Until now, our destiny may have been dull; but tomorrow could say another tale. And overnight, we can take back a current feeling of fulfillment. An old Greek proverb says, "Call no guy pleased until he's dead." In the middle of life itself, the final judgment on the quality of our lives cannot be created. It can, therefore, never be done. We anticipate this, however. Here's an obvious instance of dealing with an issue before all the data is available.

Because our existential decisions can always be rejected, it's always too early to do it. If these constantly timely evaluations are beneficial, only unnecessary calculations are wasteful for some moment. The outcome can be disastrous if they are unfavorable. The key characteristic of chronic depression is premature adverse assessments throughout existence. In the extreme, they contribute to murder, which is the most anticipatory of all. Suicide feels down to its very end in the labyrinth of the moment, finding nothing worth staying in there.

What he ignored is that he can alter his data. Although his desperation is based on an existential doubt as to the very intent of human life, tomorrow, next year, or 20 years from now, that doubt can be solved in an unimaginable manner. But suicide now chooses that it is never going to occur.

He must look at it from a perspective beyond his own mortality, in order to make such a judgment through all his lives and opportunities. This brings him to the ultimate point of advancing.

The questions concerning the nature of existence in its entirety are always early, as we never finish living. This does not imply that we should not always ask them. After all, they are intriguing analytical and conjectural subjects. However, it's always too early to resolve a reply.

The third punishment is in vain because we missed the importance of the objective before reaching it. We buy theater tickets one week beforehand, although, for all play, the theater is half full. And then, on the designated day, we are called out of the city, or we become sick, or we read such an overview that we lose all wish to be present. We are now stuck with valuable tickets. In this case, it is not a case of having been more difficult than necessary to achieve the goal or of having to do the work again to secure the goal. It is in our ownership of what was guaranteed.

However, it loses importance. In the first location, nothing had to be done. We've been working in vain. If every achievement was sold out, we should have taken our opportunity or abandoned the concept of continuing straight from the beginning. As it is, by delaying our acquisition to the last minute, we would have run no risk. It has not functioned alone in vain that helps us anticipate our actions. The danger of working in vain has risen in no way.

We often end up working in vain because we care about our issues. If he doesn't return to our table in five minutes, then we immediately discover him, smiling and apologizing, contemplated what to tell an attending waiter. After struggling for years, we unexpectedly inherit a fortune to be financially autonomous. Our thoughts and fights were in vain. It is impossible to totally ignore the possibility that the objective will be lost before we reach it, as is the risk of finding our job unworked. Again, however, it is useless to unnecessarily boost this danger. Nothing causes us to disregard a careless waiter until we are prepared to face him. By working five minutes in advance, we can't take benefit that the issue goes away without lifting our finger. On the other side, in the hope of getting a questionable heritage, it is dangerous to laze. We are the worst to have waited until the last time before we can deal with the problem if the customer remains watching us. But if the heritage we relied on does not come our way, we are deeply in difficulty.

Work is strongly linked to the persistence trap in vain. The distinction is temporary, just like overworking and amplifying. We operate towards an objective that has lost its significance when we continue. If we operate in vain, we aim for an objective that loses its significance before we get it. We can never understand until after the reality that we work in vain. The trap does not improve the likelihood of this case in any way.

Some conditions seem to call for more than one type of trapped thinking. One of these happens when we are faced with a danger we can't prevent. We may be unsustainably concerned about our imminent misfortune in this scenario and in which event we will fall into a fixed trap. We can also engage in a way that leads to us being unprofitable. In our pre-resignation job, we so that we can embrace the feared incident equally. We operate in our ideas and emotions.

Threatened with a visit by a sad friend, we reassure ourselves that the night will quickly be over, and tomorrow is a day that will give personality to pain. In brief, before it overtakes us, we surrender ourselves to our destiny.

Pre-resignation is definitely not as ineffective as a mere concern. If the worst happens, we will feel better than we have retired. But the worst can't happen— our friend can get down to influenza — and then we'll get dim for nothing. Our job is going to be in vain.

As with all operations aimed at a potential purpose, whether such a job is a trap relies on the fact that it is possible to postpone it unpaid. The imminent calamity may leave us in such a weak state that the internal funds to take over our destiny are no longer available. In that situation, we must evaluate the comparative benefit of dismissal against the likelihood of working in vain. But after the reality, it's generally just as simple to leave. When our relative is firmly in the living room, we can excuse ourselves for a moment, go to the bedroom and make our peace as much as possible. Certainly, we'll work in vain far more often than we need if we get used to getting ready for the worst always. Usually, there is enough moment to embrace our destiny when it overtakes us. Instead of being constantly dim by assuming that the worst is always the case, we would be safer not to assume that we are living our lives. If the bad thing happens, we can see what we are going to do.

Anticipation has a main feature with the fixation trap. We are unnecessarily interested in the future in both pits. The distinction is that we only live in the future in fixation without trying to build on it. Our work should be productive in advance, but it is early and thus likely to overwork, prework, and work without success. If we are troubled that we will not find our missing wallet on the lost, we are fixing. We're expecting that if we plan to substitute our missed driving license and library card before we reach the lost one. These plans may demonstrate helpful, as opposed to just worrying. But we would do better to put them off until we learned if they were needed. Anticipation is not as senseless as fearing and other types of fixation, as anticipation is at least likely to be helpful.

However, a not - so-sense forecast may form the basis for an irreparably senseless fixation. After we have started too quickly, we may not do anything before we can complete the project. We're just tempted to sit and wait, then. The customers are scheduled to arrive several hours prior to their arrival, and we will begin our party preparatory activities too soon in the day. If we hadn't expected, we wouldn't have been able to fix ourselves.

The longer we anticipate, the greater the possibility of subsequent fixation. We risk giving up unnecessary considerations on the forthcoming undertaking the week if we pack for a journey a week too early. It's like we've gone now. And if we pack two weeks too quickly, two weeks before the body can obey, we take our mental break.

At the other time extreme of the same phenomenon, we anticipate a few moments and then fix it on for a few moments until we again catch a tide of events. We get up on the bus from our seat— and stay by the gate for a while. If we still have a block away from the front door, we bring our home key out and keep it in front of us prepared to take action while we travel on the road. Several people stood at the gate of a bus with their keys in hand to look for the whole globe as if they were planning to open a cab to let themselves out. These momentary flukes are not very significant in themselves. But they considered a more particular mind habit, which interferes severely with ideal functioning. The individual who gets his keys too early, who comes too early and stays at the airport, is the same individual. Instead of acting timely and appropriate to the situation, she follows a strict model as quickly as the assignment is defined, as far as possible at this late stage, and then waits still until she can proceed again. This mechanical conduct would be expected from an easy robot, which was constructed to turn buttons in locks and to and from airports. Such a machine could go to the airport immediately and switch off until the next lap. It doesn't have to do anything else.

We're never as likely to anticipate that we will prepare timetables and future plans. True, we often must work out what to do afterward. However, scheduling can also be early, like any other type of job. Plans too early are overworked as they take into consideration opportunities that will eliminate themselves in time. You will probably be decreased to work due to evolving conditions that force us to revise our hopes. In that event, the job of scheduling has been in vain; they can demonstrate totally pointless. The longer we wait for our schedules, the less probable it is that we will have these fatalities. We can't delay forever, of course. Like all other types of jobs, there is a moment when we will be injured by further delays. This item can be defined accurately in the event of schedules. The moment to lay down our future intentions is when they will influence what we are to do now. If the dentist invites us to come in for an inspection, we have to create a scheme straight away because the recipient requires a response now. If we're planning an exit to the golf course, we might have to plan the remainder of the week to see if we can afford it now. What we are doing now may rely on our future intentions. We would not ask for medical school now if we did not want in a few years to become a doctor.

However, plans which have no impact on our current activities are anticipatory. We don't need them by definition. It doesn't matter whether we plan to get up to work or amuse ourselves when we eat dinner the following half-hour. It doesn't matter now. We will eat that soup, that entrée, and then that dessert in either event. After lunch, the choice can wait. It should wait, therefore. We can be taught about an unforeseen and beautiful chance to have fun after lunch. And then our work schedules were drawn up in vain.

Of all living conditions, when we're already engaged in a precious activity, we need the least strategy for the future. Until the assignment is obviously required or desired, the scheduling may be delayed until we finish it without a punishment. It's enough to understand that this is a good time. It is time to look forward to the future. We can't do anything about it anyway. We are already busy. We already are busy.

However, the most common of all psychic traps is to decide what to do next before the assignment is completed. We decide what to do with lunch when driving back from the job. We intend to watch TV in the evening during lunch. We arrange the job the next morning watching television. We expect dinner at a job. At job. We reflect upon the company of the evening at dinner. We are considering moving back in the evening... This curious practice could be called a one-step advance.

Chapter 3

Solving the Problem

A one-thousand-mile trip begins with a step-whether it is a mistake you made yesterday, your concern about your work/school performance at the moment, or your concern about your future and where you are going to be career-oriented is always a current component of our life. The journey is thousands of miles. Modern life has more stress in every corner than ever before; leaving us in a permanent state of stress and combat-or-flight reaction on the same point as a scenario of life-or-death because your brain does not make any distinction between adverse mental and physical stimulation (e.g., jobs, friendships, so's, finance, schools, family, kids etc.). Due to continual pressure, anxiety, concern, fear, and overthrow can easily be overcome; in an effort to get along with it and find an alternative. However, the stress is usually too much to bear and consumes you entirely. It does not contribute to this contest, the expectations of society, the social media, or self-help guides, like this one, that portrayed an idealized American dream lifestyle (e.g., wealthy individuals, cars, housing, SOs, holidays, fine dining) that everybody felt forced to follow. This fear of failure can be attributed back to college during our formation years only to the extent that thought will generate anxiety and anxiety in individuals. Childhood trauma caused by violence and negligence also makes an enormous contribution to the overthrow by the fact that the affected person is continually in a stressful state, so as to react to any future threats.

Overthinking happens when you get older and when you are overcharged with rational and real data in your curious childlike brains. Our brains were at the peak of curiosity when we were kids, creating billions of links every minute and getting data. This interest in innovative and original environments, such as art or music, is essential. Since the response to creativity is neither correct nor incorrect, kids are free to discover their own wonders without being imprisoned for their own alternatives. Author and advisor for the global education Sir Kenneth Robinson thinks that when kids join the official college scheme, they stop getting the drive to discover their own response. Robinson's Ted Talk offers an anecdotal instance of a woman in an art class who takes the danger of answering an unidentified query creatively: What does God feel like?

"She was six, and she was sitting behind, writing, and the teacher said that she seldom ever took care of it, but she did this class in drawing. The professor was fascinated, and she passed to her and wondered,' What do you draw? The maestro said,' No one understands how god appears.' And the kid said,' They'll take a photo of God in the minute.' Six years old, she had still the greatest level of curiosity. The kid said,' They'll be painting a photo of God.' She did not understand what God feels like, yet, regardless of its legitimacy, she feels sure of her depiction. Robinson claims that the education scheme made us afraid of failure both in college and particularly in the life, due to the fear of failure, specific degrees of achievement, and a single concentrate on scholastical ability and the unique purpose of having a job. Creative, childish ideas, like God's understanding by the girl, are substituted by enormous quantities of concrete information, either right or ungrateful. As children learn to fear being mistaken, they don't share their artistic thoughts with everybody else anymore. Robinson claims it removes pure and unconstrained creativity. That's why we've overthought. Our years of formation are full of teaching, both in and outside of the college. We always get fresh data from all environments, such as our own environments, colleagues, and relatives. This can be good, but only to a certain extent. Dr. Barry Schwartz suggests in his novel "The Parody of Choice," that it is essential for individuals to think that their choices are accessible when they decide about their lives. And only by obtaining expertise and information can we know about a wider spectrum of decisions than we presently have. However, this can contribute to an overload of data, so we get bored. Our decision-making method is reduced when there are seemingly numerous choices. So, if our college system offers us a weighty amount of data and we are afraid that we are incorrect and if we continually take a fresh view and thoughts for the way we live, overthinking seems inevitable. We always want to pick the correct route, and we have too many choices. The psychologist Susan Nolen-Hoeksema said that overthinking is a natural and hardwired force in our heads. All our memories, ideas, and feelings are linked as part of the neural network. While this neural web network certainly strengthens our ability to think, it also makes us more likely to overthink.

Now that you have a better understanding of the possible causes of rethinking, you will discover how to keep it dead in its path. Firstly, it is essential to remember that rethinking is an automatic practice, which you are not fully aware of because it is mainly due to a knee-jerk reaction from your corps to any type of adverse stimulation. Consider psychiatric assistance, if needed, if you are a child abuse victim. Childhood trauma is a severe disorder deep in the psyche that makes it hard to cure without skilled assistance. There are 10 easy and efficient techniques and advice to stop thinking and bring your lives back under command:

1. **Remember that you don't learn more by thinking too much.**

You would need a degree of understanding of each choice in order to comprehend what choice is best. However, it makes no sense to think through this logically. Why is that? Because you never understand precisely what will happen until you do it.

School, move back, marry, end a friendship, change profession. However, much you feel your lives will alter; you will be amazed by the results of these monumental events. You can live lives with a real knowledge of what you can do if you know. Action leads rather than thinking about clarity.

2. **Your decision can be changed**

Often it is a conviction that your choice is final, that your choice will stay the same and always right. It's a question of over-thinking. This will not occur. It will not occur. This is good. And that is good. Would it be worth living if you could forecast your whole future completely? All the thrill of life is taken back. You have to remember that your choice may be incorrect, regardless of how critical you thought about it. Take convenience in the likelihood of error and realize that you change your views and understandings of the present scenario over moment will lead to an understanding of real internal liberty and serenity.

3. Know why you get hurt and let it push you to fresh heights by thinking over.

Research has shown that rumination is strongly associated with depression, anxiety, binge eat, binge drink, and self-harm. The most significant stress forecaster, accompanied by family history, earnings and education, state of the partnership, and social inclusion, was the case with 32,827 individuals from 172 nations, one research found.

But the research also showed that stress only occurs if the person has overthought about occurrences badly and shows that individuals, although they have had much adverse stuff, have not become stressed or depressed. So, care about your issues, but be ready to deal with pressure or depression implications.

4. Avoid being Idle

Make sure that both your mind and body are occupied during the day because you have too much free time, the primary reason for overthinking. If time is allocated to pointless thinking, a day cannot be worthwhile. A mind can sleep well in the evening, knowing that its day is worthwhile. Get your heart and blood pumps on a regular basis— all physical activity. Walking, sports, Pilates, and even practicing with your pet can include simple and efficient practices. You don't like an Olympic competitor have to work out. Just move as a beginning.

5. Be thoroughly skeptical.

If you think about what makes thinking so exhausting, nervous, and exhausting, our private judgments generally make our ideas fully true. An example: if a known person does something unkind, but you do not take the question to his attention, then you can think badly about why they did that nasty thing. Here's the example. But after I find out which ideas cause this; a matter of armor drives away all negativity: "I can 100% rest assured that my mind is real?" It automatically calms rates you in cases by recognizing the inherent reality losses of your convictions, and you will not over-think the anticipations and hypothesis.

6. But don't vent, look for assistance. Find assistance.

Seek the help and guidance of loved ones instead of basing your decisions on your own prejudices, point of view, and mental lens. Research has shown that social support has a strong long-term impact on stress relief. You will also have an initial and fresh view on a subject. This has always led to unpredictable teaching experience in every event. That's how someone matures spiritually and mentally.

7. Learn how to Forgive

It's no surprise that being disrespectful results in disregard for others. It's not surprising that being unrespectful outcomes. Pardon is one of the highest qualities of mankind. Not because it is moral, spiritually created, or a worthy character, but because it can generate the supreme peace on its own. Forgiveness has shown a great deal of favorable self-esteem, increased mood, and an enormous margin to enhance health. It predicts health and marriage relationships and has been connected to a longer life span.

8. Introduce your life with deliberate diversion

How long do you ruminate? Have you ever taken this issue into consideration? It's after a job or college for most individuals in the evening.

You can plan a massive event in this free time slot if you understand what moment to ruminate. E.g., sudoku, board match, eat out, yoga, or write lovely letters to invisible buddies.

Please notice: some study suggests that this can have damaging, long-term implications through damaging reinforcement behavior, such as toxic food plans. Choose your diversion closely and make sure your psychological and emotional health is good.

9. First, for view, solve somebody's issues.

The slogan for anybody who is presently disturbed by his own perceive issues should be "serve first, want a second. Your issues can be so overwhelming that others will feel that you live in your own globe, and you need something to break out. You are reminded by assisting others that everyone is in difficulty, some of them more than ever before. This is not to discredit your own battles, but to help others to restore equilibrium and order back to life.

10.   A bold decision is not always the right one

You know, the perfect choice is not a courageous choice—get started today When you reach the crevice of your life, you will never worry about how well your choices are well thought through, or how you have been through the forks in the way of life completely and successfully. You will be happy to know that you have lived true to yourself, have taken self-assurance, and stand up for your convictions. Don't care if your choices were ideal or not. Although you might be heading momentarily in the wrong direction, be sure always to move forward. Timidity is admirable; caution never altered anything. You can begin regaining control of your worried mind with these easy policies. Last but not least, your own fear would be dropped, and you would start to live in the true globe again. Long-term alternatives will be discussed in the next section for overthinking.

Chapter 4

Long Term Solutions

"They just fix nothing, stress, and care. It is blocking creativity. You can't even believe in the alternatives. Susan L. Taylor: Short-term policies and pieces of advice for preventing transient overthinking have been discussed in the past section; other longer-term alternatives you can use in your lives will be discussed in this section. These include altering your viewpoint, breaking down self-destructive practices, and relaxation. First and foremost, we will examine how to alter your viewpoint, in particular, how to recognize the insecurity and chaos in life that makes everything unnecessary. This can be achieved by means of one branch of life philosophy: Stoicism.

The Stoicism, created in Athens by Zeno of Citium at the beginning of the 3rd century BC and known as the philosophy of Epictetus, the Seneca, and emperor Marcos Aurelius. A brief summary and definition of this Hellenistic school. Stoicism. This philosophy is that goodness (for example, knowledge) is gladness, and judgment is not words. It also teaches us that we control nothing and cannot count on internal events (e.g., luck, god, destiny).

Stoicism just has to know a few key courses. It reminds us of the unpredictability of the globe. How brief is our life how to be solid, powerful, and in control, particularly when it comes to mental display? Finally, our dissatisfaction is not because of the difficult logic but rather because of our impulsive reliance on our unintentional emotions.

Stoicism does not depend on the complicated world hypothesis but helps us to overcome destructive feelings and act when possible. It's for intervention, not for discussion.

There were three leading figures. The Emperor of the Romans, Mario Aurelius, then the strongest person in the world, sat down every day to compose notes concerning discipline, compassion, and humility. He endured slavery in order to begin his own college, in which many of Rome's biggest minds were tutored. Seneca only believed about his wife's and friends ' consolations when Nero cheated him and demanded his suicide because he was willing to embrace death by adopting stoicism.

But these are not all three — Kings, presidents, painters, authors, and businessmen have used story-wide storytelling. Stoicism is used in both the past and the present.

In his saddlebags, the Prussian, Frederick the Grand, allegedly traveled with the Stoic doctrines, "carrying you through misery," in his words. In the meantime, the politician and essayist Montaigne had a row of Epictetus sculpted over his research, where most of his moment was wasted.

This philosophy also influenced the founding fathers. George Washington was informed by his friends of the Stoicism at 17, and subsequently, he placed Cato to a game to raise the hopes of his men in the Valley Forge in the summer, whereas Seneca's job on his bed stand had Thomas Jefferson at the time of his death.

The ideas of economist Adam Smith regarding worldwide integration— capitalism — were influenced by the stoicism of a professor, Marcus Aurelius, who researched as a kid.

In a famous essay on Liberty, political thinker John Stuart Mill has written about Marcus Aurelius and Stoicism, remarking that it is "the greatest ethical result of the old mind." Stoicism, rather than academic brothers, is in a core manner distinct from most current colleges. This is an instrument we can use to make stronger friends and individuals in our job.

Stoicism is nearer than a novel of philosophy that a professor of the university could submit to a pre-game warm-up. It prepares for philosophical existence, where it's most essential to have the correct framework. Stoics performed "religious exercises" from which power stemmed. Let's look at nine of the major workouts.

1. Engage yourself in Misfortune

"It's time for safety that the spirit should prepare for hard moments; while money gives favors, it's time to reinforce it against its rebuffs." — Seneca, a Nero counselor with excellent riches, proposed that we should exercise the diet a few days a month. Eat little nutrition, wear your ragged dresses, and leave the house and sleep convenience. "There's something I used to fear, confront wants head-on," he said, you'll question yourself. "Remember, this is a real practice; it is essential. It's not only "thinking about" poverty, but it's also about experiencing it. Comfort imprison you for fear of something or someone taking it from you always. It's a comfort. But if you can't just expect but also misfortune, then chance can't destroy your existence anymore.

Montaigne had an old drinking game, where everyone turned around carrying a corpse painting in a coffee and cheering, "Drink and be happy for you to look like this when you're dead." Emotions such as anxiety or dread have their roots in uncertainty and are usually true to their knowledge. Anybody who bets a lot on himself understands how much energy or fear he can eat. The answer is for ignorance to be addressed. Get acquainted with the worst-case situations you fear.

Practice in your mind or in actual existence what you're afraid of. It's nearly always correct or short-lived.

2. Train your mind to disregard good and bad

"Do not choose to harm, and you will never think hurt." Don't feel hurt, and you're not. -Marcus Aurelius Stoics had an activity called Turning the Upside Down of the Obstacle. The aim was to prevent philosophy from being practiced. Because every poor one becomes positive if you can correctly spin an issue on your head.

Suppose you try to help someone for one second and react by being reluctant or reluctant to work together. Rather than tighten your lives, the workout tells you that you are directed at fresh qualities, like patience or comprehension. Or, someone's mortality at your edge; a chance to show natural virtue.

Marcus Aurelius portrayed this as follows: "The obstacle to intervention promotes intervention. The way forward is what the technique represents. "This should be familiar as a consequence of the thought behind Obama's" teachable times. "Joe Klein questioned Obama just before the contest how he developed his call to react to the Wright Reverend Scandal. He said,' when the tale was bad, and I could not do what was most efficient, it was to speak with Americans like adolescents.' And he ended up converting an adverse situation into the perfect platform for his remarkable racial discourse.

The prevalent practice of entrepreneurs is that they take benefit of possibilities, even generate them. In the Stoic, it's all a chance. The Reverend Wright scandal, a frustrating case in which the death of a loved one is unappreciated by your facilitators, is not "opportunities" within the traditional meaning of the word. They're the other. It's a barrier. What a Stoic is doing is turning every barrier into an opportunity.

Effective Stoic is not nice or harmful. The only understanding exists. You control awareness. You can extrapolate your original feeling afterward (' X occurred.'–>' X occurred, and my life is over now.'). You will find that everything is only a chance by tying your first response to unemotionality.

3. Remember, it is all Ephemeral

"Alexander the Great with his jack everybody died, and therefore everyone feels the same thing."— Marcus Aurelius. Marcus Aurelius wrote a simple and efficient reminder of him to help him recover his outlook and maintain healthy:" Run down the list of those who feel intensive wrath for anything. Smoke, dirt, legend... or not a myth. Please consider all the instances. It is essential to note that "passion" here is not a trendy consumption that we are at home with, like with excitement or care for something. And how insignificant are the things we want, like this stormy region? When the Stoics address overcoming the' passions' they call' Patricia,' they speak of the unreasonable, unhealthy, and exaggerated wishes and feelings. Wrath would be a nice case in point. The most significant thing to remember is that they try, instead of unnecessary enjoyment, to substitute eupathy for them. Back to the workout level, it's easy: nevertheless, remember small you zone unit. However, note that most of them are small. Recall that accomplishments are transitory and only a moment your possession is.

What matters if all is ephemeral? That is right now. That's what counts, and this is essential for Stoics as a good man and doing the right thing straight away.

Take Alexander, the United Nations Great Agency captured the globe and had appointed towns. This is the understanding of the public. The Stoics also wanted to see that Alexander had once been drunk and inadvertently murdered Alexander, with his beloved friend Cleitus. Later he got so hot that for 3 days, he wasn't able to eat or drink. Sophists from across the Balkans were called to examine in vain what they could do about his grief. Is this an indication of success? From a personal view, if you lose view and harm those around you, it counts little when your name is emblazoned on a map.

Learn from the error of Alexander. Be lowly, frank, and conscientious. Every day of your lives, that's something you can have. It never takes someone from you or, worse, it takes you over. You'll never have to worry about someone.

4. Take the view from a height

"How beautifully Plato put it. " Whenever you'd like to talk about people, it's better to look at the bird's eye and see all of them at the same time— meetings, military groups, farms, marriages and divorce, births and fatalities, bruises, or quiet spaces, every strange person, every holiday, commemorative place, every market, all of them combined with each other. This practice—which involves millions of individuals, "troops, farms, marriages and divorces, births and deaths," all of us—leads us to look ahead and reminds us, however small we tend to have an area unit, a little like the past exercise. It turns us on, and as a Stoic scientist, Pierre Hadot puts it, "the perspective of stuff from higher up is more than changing the way our value decisions look: luxury, authority, war... and concerns about living standards become ridiculous." The second, more sophisticated goal is to explore Stoics or a shared interdependence with humanity as a whole. "In the outer space you create a global awareness of, a tendency towards the peoples, an intense discontent with the state of the globe and the obligation to do something about it" (Second View from Abbaum) As the astronaut King of Great Britain Mitchell puts a real' opinion from above,' Grab the perspective of Plato.

5. Memento Mori: Mortality meditation

"Let us prepare our minds as if we are back to the terrible end of existence." Let us postpone anything. Nothing. Every day let's balance books of life. Seneka, the quote from Seneca above, takes half the reminder of Mori — the ancient sequel to the philosopher's reflection on mortality, who previously stated that the correct follow-up of philosophy is "about nothing but death and dying." Marcus Aurelius, in his Meditations, wrote that "you can leave but die and be dead." That was a private reminder that you now live a life of faith and do not wait. It was an invitation to live a life of freedom.

Your death meditation is only depriving if you skip the goal. The Stoics think this idea revives and does not make sense. It is no surprise that Dying is a regular name in every biography of Seneca. After all, it is Seneca who urged America to let us know that "Maybe you won't wake up tomorrow," when we go to bed and "Maybe you won't sleep again." Or as another Stoic, Epictetus, beg his learners: "Maintain death and exile before your eyes every day and everything that seems awful — this will never lead you to a basic idea, nor can you want excessively." Use these reminders and meditate on them each day — let them be the construction blocks of existence to the full and not to waste a second.

6. Can I control this?

The primary job in life is merely this: to locate and divide things into different areas, so I will obviously state to myself that external areas of the unit are not managed by me and that they have to do with the options I really manage. Where can I seek sensitivity and bad then? to external decision-making, not uncontrollable ones, but my own ones within myself. The only major exercise in Stoic philosophy is to differentiate between what we can modify and what we cannot. What we tend to be influential about and do not do. The weather causes a plane to be postponed—no number of shouts can end a tempest at AN's airline official. There can be no desire in an extremely distinct nation that can make you larger, smaller, or born. You can't create someone like you, no matter how tedious you're trying. And in addition, time spent shouting at these immovable items isn't spent on the things we can change.

Return to this issue every day in every attempt. Review and constantly think about it. If you can focus on clearly identifying what elements in your daylight unit and the elements that don't seem to be in your management, you won't be happy just; you have some benefit compared to other UN agencies that don't understand that they are fighting NO unprofitable struggle.

7. A Diary

The slave's diary Epictetus. The emperor Marcus Aurelius. The playwright and power broker Seneca. These three {radically different} people diode completely distinct life.

However, they seemed to have one prevalent practice: journaling.

Each of them did it in one way or another. It would be Epictetus UN organization to warn its learners that philosophy is one thing they "must write down day by day." Seneca's favorite journaling moment was the nighttime. Only then would he go to bed, discovering "that the sleep that follows this self-examination" to be considered nice. He said to a colleague, "Throughout my lifetime, I look and go home and say nothing; nothing hid from me; nothing went by." And Marcus was the most prodigious of journalists, and we are happy to have his texts, properly named, "To himself," "To him." In Stoicism, journalistic art is more than simply a diary. It's not only a simple diary. It's a good idea to use a diary of his works. The philosophy is this regular exercise. The day ahead is in preparation. The day that went by reflects. It reminds us of the wisdom that our lecturers, our reading, and our experience tend to teach us. It is not enough to simply hear those lessons once; instead, you practice them over and over, turn them into your mind and, above all, write them down and feel them flowing through your fingers. This is how Stoicism is reported. It can hardly have one while not the other way around.

8. Practice Visualizing a Negative Image

The premeditation Malorum is a Stoic practice in the imagination of stuff that may fail or be quarantined from us. Practice Negative visual image It enables us to prepare for the unavoidable retrogressions of life. Even if we gained it, we do not constantly get what is really ours. It is not all as tidy and simple as we expect it to be. We ought to prepare for this psychologically. It is one of the strongest exercises in the Stoic kit to generate power and resilience. For example, Seneca would first re-examine or re-examine his intentions, say, to visit. And then he would go through (or prevent it from happening in the leader's head, as we have mentioned above), the things which could be {failed would} — a tempest may occur, the skipper may fall ill, the vessel may be pirated.

"The wise person does nothing against his expectation," he told a friend.' Nothing occurs against his expectations. ". Nevertheless, he thought that one thing could block his plans, "he said in particular. By doing this practice, Seneca was constantly prepared to interrupt him and always worked on his plans. He was ready to win or defeat.

9. AMOR FATI: Love All the Things that Happen

The excellent German thinker Friedrich the philosopher would define his recipe of human grandeur as Cupid Fati— a love of destiny. "You don't want anything entirely distinct, not forward, not back, not forever. Not just to bear what's essential, but to disguise it less.... but to enjoy it. "However, not only were the Stoics at home from this view. Two thousand years agonized Emperor Marcus Aurelius would tell in his own personal diary called Meditations: "A burning fire causes fire and luminosity out of all that is tossed into its fire." Another Stoic, Epictetus who, as an attentive slave, is lunar adversely affected by adversity, echoes the same: "Do not strive for the events to occur as you want them to be; Not only to be all right with it, but also to enjoy it and be greater. So that barriers and adversity become fuel for your future, like elements in a chimney.

Stoicism is Ideal for the Important World

The Stoics wrote honestly and often autocratically; however, they can be higher folks, be content and handle the issues they faced. Stoicism is ideal for a significant world. However, in the presence of adversity, you can see active misfortune strengthening; however, turning AN obstacle upwards transforms the problem into possibilities {and yet the way} the fundamental cognition method holds your ego manageable and in view as small as yourself.

This is Stoicism at the end of the day. It's not about why or how the universe is systematically discussed. It's a number of recalls, advice and helps to lead a healthy life.

Stoicism is not, as Marcus remembers, a big instructor but a bazoid, a relaxing ointment for an accident, in which we may have an accident. Epictetus was correct when he said: "Life is exhaustive, cruel, punishing, restricting, and confining, a deadly affair." We should do nothing to enhance our ability to reach, and this will simply help us. Now, as the Stoicism and its practicality of today have been addressed, we will proceed to the strength of practices and the crucial part of how and how it works.

A youthful female enters a lab. She has almost converted every aspect of her life over the previous two years. She stopped smoking, went to work for a marathon, and was promoted. Neurologists find that the models inside her brain have changed radically — Procter & Gamble marketers research videos of individuals who create their beds. The business is desperately trying to find a manner to promote a substitution item called Febreze, one of the most significant flops in the history of the business. Suddenly, one detects a nearly unnoticeable model — and Febreze earns billions of USD a year with a tiny change in marketing. One of the largest companies in America is taken over by a not tested chief operating officer. His first company order is an attack on his employees— as regards safety for employees— and the company, Alcoa, is currently the top inventory performers. What are all these individuals together? By specializing in the designs that make up each part of our life, they have accomplished achievement. The practices were successful.

The Habit Schoon is a habit-regulating neurological model. It has three features: a cue, a routine, and a recompense. The knowledge of these elements will, however, help to understand how to change hazardous practices or sensitive types. A cue, a trigger that moves the brain into a mode that determines that practice of use automatically, always begins. Mental, emotional, or physical exercise could be the core of your practice. In the end, there is a legacy that helps the brain check whether this particular loop is a cognitive value method for the future. Duhigg states in an essay of the New York Times: "The stick and the award are intertwined neurologically until there is a feeling of longing." Duhigg says that a desire drives all practices and is vital at the start of substitution or destruction of the latest practice. Duhigg defines what Procter and Gamble used to create the industry for Febreze, a product that eliminates poor odors to create a fortune, with an assessment of the habit loop and the relation to its cravings.

The Golden Rule of Habit Change

The Golden law of practice changes enables prevent practices and substitute them with fresh ones. The golden rule of habits changes. It states that change could take place if you maintain the initial indication, replace the routine, and preserve the reward, although the UN agency doesn't believe that what they do is able to appear to disappoint the expectations and to provide. Belief is a critical aspect of such a change, although it is organized into a wide range of environments and clusters. Often UN agencies are more contented than those who behave as individuals by themselves, like responsible teams in the region. Charles Duhigg used several instances to explain his reasoning, including the situation of Bill Wilson, an alcoholic recovering whose fresh faith diode him to be an NGO in Christ. He also stated the' power of will' in the novel and its part in becoming a practice.

Keystone Habits

A cornerstone habit is an employee model that can inadvertently trigger distinct behaviors in a person's life. Duhigg told Alcoa that it was in a situation to leverage the company's capital by $27 billion by promoting safety in the working environment. He also told the chief operations officer Paul H. O'Neill. O'Neil said, "I realized I needed to turn Alcoa, [b], but you cannot command the people to change it, but that's not how the brain operates. So, I've always thought I'm starting out with a single problem. If I can start to disrupt the practices around a problem, that's going to stretch throughout the company."

Relaxation is a term that is often used in many different societies to describe a range of sentiments, emotions, and conduct. It is related to pleasures, control and self-assurance, laughter, feelings, calm and tranquility, relaxation, exercise, massage, bathing, musical listening, eating, alcohol drinking, and relaxation. Healthcare professionals and laypersons in the same region frequently understand the advantages of relaxation in health through papers, textbooks, and scientific journals in the popular media, but it is often uncertain what relaxation is implied by what techniques to pick and how to move.

1. Meditate

Meditate a couple of minutes per day will make anxiety easier. "Research suggests that meditation on a regular basis may modify the neural routes of the brain and make you more stress-resistant," tells psychologist Robbie Maller Hartman, Ph.D.

This is easy. It is easy. Sit up directly on the floor with two feet. Just close your eyes. Close your eyes. Place a hand on your stomach and synchronize your name with your breaths. Simply focus on reiterating—noisy or still—a favorable mantra such as "I feel at ease" or "I enjoy myself" Allow distracting ideas like clouds to fly.

2. Take Deep Breaths

Take a short break, say for like 5-minutes, and concentrate on your respiration. Sit directly, your eyes shut, your stomach with aside. Little by little, inhale into your nose and feel the breath beginning in your abdomen and push its way up to your neck. Turn the method back on as you exhale.

"The impacts of stress are countered by delay and lowered pressure rates by depth diving," claims psychologist Judith

Tutin, Ph.D. She is a Life Coach licensed in Rome, GA. 3. Be present slow down. Be present slow down.

3. Be Present

Tutin suggests: "Take 5 minutes and concentrate on only one conscious behavior." Notice, but when you walk, the wind touches on your face, and how your feet feel hitting the base. Enjoy each slice of meat in its texture and style. You should feel less uncomfortable if you receive time and specialize in your emotions.

4. Reach Out

Reaching out is one of your greatest ways to handle the pressure. Speak to others—or perhaps on the telephone, ideally. Share what happens. Share what happens. You can take the latest view while maintaining your membership robust.

5. Tune in your Body

Mind-screen your body to see how stress impacts your body every day. Sit with your feet on the floor, lie on your side. Start with your fingers and operate with your skin, and see how your body works.

"Simply know where you feel narrow or loose without trying to change something," suggests Tutin. Imagine every deep breath going into that portion for 1 to a couple of minutes. Repeat this method as your focus is shifted up, and the emotions you experience in each portion pay close attention.

6. Decompress

Please place a hot heat cloth for ten minutes around your throat and shoulders. Close your eyes and ease the bones of your face, neck, top of the chest, and back. Remove the cover and massage stress by using a tennis ball or a foam roller.

"Set your back and the wall in the box. Stick in the field and keep the stress low for up to 15 seconds. Then push the stick and exert pressures, "said Cathy Benninger, a nurse and professor at the Wexner University in Columbus, Ohio State.

7. Laugh out Loud

A good belly laugh doesn't just mentally lighten the burden. It reduces cortisol, the stress hormone of your body, and stimulates brain chemicals called endorphins that make your mood easier for you. Smiling, reading comics, or talking to somebody at the UN organization, enhanced by listening to your favorite program or video.

8. Crank up the tunes

Research demonstrates a reduction of stress, heart rate, and anger by listening to relaxing music. "Get your mind to specialized in the different parts, tools, and performers in this song and create a playlist of places and sounds (the sea, a bubble-broom, chirping birds)." You're going to steam away by rolling dead and put on lots of beautiful songs—or sing on top of your lung!

9. Get Moving

You don't need to work to cause a runner to be heavy. You need not work. All types of practice, including yoga and biking, can alleviate depression and anxiety by providing the brain with unhardened feel-good chemicals. You can choose to wander around the building quickly, take the steps up and down many rows, or do activities such as head-rolls and shoulder-shrugs.

10.   Be grateful

To maintain in mind the many things that make up this region in your lives (one by your bed, one in your bag, and one on the job). Joni Emmerling, a wellness coach in Greenville, NC, said: "I am thankful for your blessing and cancel adverse ideas and worries." Use these papers to enjoy nice experiences like the smile on a child, the day full of sun, and excellent health. Don't forget to celebrate achievements such as a job substitution assignment or a fresh hobby.

When you get upset, waste a couple of minutes looking through your notes to find out what is highly important to you. Sleep, which has a vital function in teaching, memory, and anxiety management, is as essential as relaxation. Research shows that sleep has an important function to play in memory before and when teaching a fresh job. Missing sleep has an impact on mood, motivation, judgment, and our perception of occurrences.

Although some open questions concerning sleep's accurate function in the formation and storage of reminiscences exist, there is overall agreement that fortified sleep is ideal for teaching and memory throughout the evening.

Sleep and the Learning Process

Healthy sleep is crucial for effective teaching and memory functioning.

Sleep, education, and memory units have progressed, not fully grasped phenomena. Animal and human trials show, however, that sleep quantity and performance have a major effect on teaching and memory. Research indicates that sleep improves memory and teaching in two different respects. First, a person without sleep cannot focus their attention in an optimal fashion and thus cannot learn quickly. Second, sleep itself has a part to play in memory strengthening, which is vital to the teaching of fresh information. Although it appears that the real processes are not noticed, learning and memory are generally depicted in 3 tasks. The introduction of fresh data to the brain relates to acquisition. Consolidation is the process of stabilization of the memory. A recall is the capacity to transfer the understanding after it has been maintained (whether deliberately or unconsciously).

Each step is important for the proper operation of the memory. Acquire and remember occurs during wakefulness only. But assessment indicates that the reinforcement of the neural links that shape our memory takes place during sleep. Although no consensus is reached with regard to sleep, many scientists assume that particular brainwave features are involved in the creation of particular memory variants in the entire various phases of the sleep zone unit.

Dr. Robert Stick gold talks about sleep, teaching, and memory; however, before and during a fresh teaching situation, sleep performs a part in memory. The function of sleep in education and memory training is studied in two respects by sleep scientists. In reaction to a variety of recent duties, the first method is presented at the multiple phases of sleep (and shifts in length). The second strategy examines the influence of sleep deprivation on teaching. Deprivation of sleep can be complete (not permitted to sleep), partial (defaulting to early or late sleep) or selective (subjected to particular sleep phases).

Types of Memory and Sleep Stages

Differently varying reminiscence areas formed into fresh teaching stuff. Sleep Stages and Memory Types Scientists examine whether or not the development of{diversifying} reminiscence variations and, hence, the multiple phases of sleep are related. The oldest sleep and memory investigations focused on declarative memory that consists of information from facts or what we understand (for instance, the French capital, or what you had last evening for lunch). One study has identified an increase in quick-eye sleep or REM sleep for persons who are involved in extensive language courses. The dreaming happens most often in this sleep stage. Scientists hypothesized that the purchase of learning content was a significant part of REM sleep. Further surveys have shown that REM exercise appears involved with declarative memory procedures when the information is sophisticated and emotional, but very probably not when the information is simple and emotional.

Researchers are now predicting that profound restored sleep (SWS) plays a significant part by a method in declared memory and consolidates newly uninherited information. Results of studies of sleep / declarative memory association have been combined, and this is a continuous evaluation district. In the capacity to be taught fresh duties that require engine cooperation and efficiency, sleep performs a significant part. Research has also focused on exercise and its function in spatial memory—"how "to make one thing (e.g., driving a cycle or practicing the guitar) the fundamental behavioral process. In the strengthening of procedural memory, REM sleep seems to play an important part. Additional elements of exercise play a part: engine training relies on the number of sleeping phases, and binding variants of visual teaching tend to depend on the amount and temporality of each profound, slow-wave (SWS) and REM sleep.

Sleep Impairment in Education and Performance

The effects of a lack of sufficient sleep on teaching and memory are another region that scientists research. If our concentrate, attention, and vigilance drift in the region of sleep is poor, so information can be difficult to obtain. Overworked neurons cannot function to correctly organize the information without sufficient sleep and rest, and we lose our capacity to access previously discovered information. Furthermore, we can also affect our understanding of occurrences. As a consequence of our failure to correctly evaluate real, schedule, and choose the right conduct, we lose the capacity to make sensible decisions. The judgment is damaged. Judgment is affected. We tend to conduct less apparently in areas units because we are chronically weary of fatigue or exhaustion. The neurons do not shoot optimally, the lungs do not cool, and the organ systems of the body do not appear to be aligned. Sleep deprivation focusing delays can even cause injury or accidents.

Sleeping deprivation of low quality also has a negative effect on mood, which has implications for the teaching process. Mood changes influence our capacity to collect fresh information and recall them subsequently. Whilst acute lack of sleep impacts completely distinct individuals in a way which (and the implications seem unknown), an honest night's remainder has a powerful effect on memory and teaching.

We shift from sleep to the interrelated issue: the concentration that is necessary for every job to be successful, and that is immediately related to our sleep times and sleep quality. The capacity to concentrate one mind or topic is concentration, without anything else from the area of consciousness. Concentration The capacity to concentrate the eye is one of the main abilities you should have. Most individuals, however, lack the ability to focus. Your focus generally wanders without being able to fix it for an inexpensive quantity of moment on one topic.

This can be fixed. This is something. Like any other capacity, the capacity to concentrate is created. An individual who trains his or her mind is able to concentrate without being distracted by ideas, sounds, or anything else.

- Do you lift yourself often: how to focus on research?
- How can mistakes be avoided?
- How much efficiency can I make?
- How to enhance memory?

- How do I get confirmation outcomes?
- How can I enhance visualization?

The solution is simple, and you need to increase your concentration.

Why Does Focus matter?

There is no overestimation of the significance of concentrate. In every room of existence and for everyone, it is essential.

This ability will make you easier when you study when you are browsing, working, driving, doing the job, meditating, and anything else.

Concentration and focus are essential for:

1. Your mind controls.
2. You reject the thoughts you don't want from your mind.
3. Inner tranquility gain.
4. Free your mind from mischievous thinking.
5. Enhance your memory.
6. Enhance your study skills.
7. It works a lot quicker.

8. Make fewer errors.

9. Advancement of meditation.

10. Inventive graphic image and get faster outcomes.

11. Intuition sharpening.

12. And a great deal.

Simple Exercise to Train Your Mind to Concentrate

- Count the phrases in a novel or journal in an extraordinarily one sentence and then count it again, to make sure you have counted them properly.

- Practice this every day, multiple times a day.

- In 2 paragraphs, attempt to investigate the phrases, and then count the phrases on one entire page.

- Take the phrases mentally, with your eyes only, to improve your concentration and concentrate without informing your thumb.

- It's a fundamental practice. Although it is a simple practice, you may not easily follow it, and you will notice your mind walking and not counting. This demonstrates that you want to train your concentration abundantly.

- You use your mind every second of the day, but you want to control and concentrate on what you are doing, and it needs to be coached.

Ultimately, it is possible to resolve to overcome this by altering your self-destructive thinking and adopting a healthier one centered on stress leadership. The next section covers good thoughts and how your lives can be improved.

Chapter 5

Positive Energies and Positive Thinking

The power of positive thinking and positive positiveness is an astonishing thing that could change your life altogether. As shown in the following review: recently in The School of Greatness, I had the chance to meet Steve Weatherford, former NFL Super Bowl Champion, who was one of every most efficient punter in the globe, about his keys to achievement, which can create the distinction. A favorable mentality will help you conquer all the barriers you face. One of the greatest factors that entrepreneurs and prospective customers can extract from the sport and athletic world is that visual picture efficacy and positive thought are effective. Studies after studies indicate the strength, but life changes follow this simple one.

Most individuals don't realize that the people in this region are always learning at the top of their successful field match, feeding their hearts and minds to keep growing. One of Steve's favorite stuff is that he is lucky, in his place of the highest 1%, one of the most successful in the globe, yet in his future career (enterprise), he is moving to another problem and still learns and grows.

"Take a look at your day in detail. Make a 30-day commitment, and your lives can change. "Steve's main hack of existence is favorable self-representation. He advises you to "speak about yourself daily. Say in the afternoon,' Today will be a great day, and it may be because.'. Visualize your day in detail. Commit yourself to the practice over thirty days, and your lives may be amended. It completely visualizes every problem. Does that? Does that? No, not so. But it can make a huge difference with the sight. "You must see in your life stuff occur before you can figure it out. It is viewing. I have discovered that as an athlete, I have never been to the business industry, asking what you do not want. Because, once you have these negative thinking, they can express a lot.

"If you are in an excessively good position, your percentage of chance to punch the excellent punt is much higher, because your unit of area wonder what you want to do and what you don't want to do or do. Steve claims his strategy to life is to imagine and schedule and take benefit from Monday's impetus. "Your brain is the strongest muscle that you have."

"Every Sunday, I write down the objectives I want to achieve in every aspect of my life; I have prepared to achieve some incredible stuff. For the week, I map out and split it into days, my vision, and achievements. I assault the most on Monday. On Monday, as a consequence, my mentality, my productivity, my effectiveness lays the tone for the rest of the week.

Self-Scouting

Steve speaks about the significance of "self-scouting" or thinking about your day to look at videos of observation when a match is like a sportsman. Identify what you were likely doing well and identify objects that you did not lock and freight for the following day.

Propensity Formulae

Steve's prosperity recipe identifies what you see, keeps your concentrate, trusts your strategy, works every day and is diligent, coherent, and good because you've got your view wherever you want to be. A consistent job is the most important part of building your vision.

"For me, prosperity is a mixture of health, prosperity, appreciation, and charity, and that I gravitate towards individuals like this because I want {I want need} to do so, and I want it to share that further with other individuals." Daily Investment Steve suggests that there are everywhere dreamers. You plan to take these daily decisions, which will complement your interest over time, to get closer to your objective. People have a true disadvantage in choosing what they need 10 years from what they need now.

Make it a matter of importance to encourage and educate you about beneficial people from the UN organization.

Impact Steve claims he now wants to make a difference to people. "You will live." You will die. But what region of your lives will you do together? You cannot bring it with you. You cannot take it with you. What will you do between now and when you leave, will it affect individuals? "That's Steve's thinking:" I plan, or I am going to know, I plan to fight, I will learn. Any error you make, any weakness you have. I don't believe in failure; I just believe in ways to develop. Your zone unit does not plan to lose, else you plan to gain. You plan to know. We can all learn something from Steve's positive winner's thinking, below is a guideline for a positive attitude:

1. Question yourself as to whether you think positively

You cannot be stopped by the fear of defeat. Ask yourself,' Do I really think so?' Don't you know if you are a negative man or not? Take this wellness questionnaire, which will not only give you a positive rating but help you to determine the reverse abilities, which can best enhance your happiness and well-being. If you want to operate on performance, continue reading if somebody is a UN organization.

2. Build up your favorable data memory

Were you aware that you could be willing to improve your performance by merely storing favorable word lists? When you push your brain to use beneficial phrases often, you create these terms (and their fundamental significance) much more available, linked, and easier to use in your brain. Once you get a phrase or schedule from your memory, beneficial people can simply go back to the primary. Don't you know the word positive area unit? Thousands of phrases have been tightly evaluated by psychologists to work out how good and negative they are. In the useful term manual for adolescents and in the positive textbook for kids, I only collected useful phrases. Try this original approach if you are disturbed to think it is good. It can help your brain grow in respects that may promote the implementation of reverse positive thinking.

3. Enhance the capacity of your brain to function with positive data.

When your brain is building strong neural networks, attempt extending these networks by requesting your brain to use beneficial information in fresh respects; for instance, you may use favorable phrases AND warn you, in inverse order, an hour ago, to recall these phrases.

Or you can write those phrases on cards, and you can split them into 2 pieces, stack them all, and then you can realize the game for each card. In order for your brain to fit the term parts, you have to look for innumerable beneficial data to look for the data you are looking for. For instance, "laughter" would be diverted into "laugh" and "her" This beneficial reminder job can help you generate it when you attempt to assume that it is good.

4. Reinforce the capacity of your brain to take care of beneficial issues

Do you think of yourself as one of those people who notice the dangerous thing — such as once someone has cut you off or your food doesn't fit as much as you wanted? Then you apparently taught your brain for the negative, and your brain became very sensitive. This coaching can be incredibly hard to reverse. Train your brain to focus on the good even better. Just concentrate on useful information and turn your attention away from the negative. Do you need to make the benefits more attentive? Examine those matches of quality.

5. Make sure you have random value moments.

Did you know that you are simply going to make a difference? You most probably learned about the research of Pavlov's dog if you ever took AN intro to the science class. This is a fast update: Pavlov had a dog. To inform his dog that it was nearly feeding time, Pavlov would ring a clock. As with most animals, once he was about to get fed, Pavlov's dog would be thrilled. So, he would drool throughout the site. What occurred? What occurred? Well, suddenly, even though food isn't a donation, Pavlov's dog just began to be thrilled. Food and the bell's noise were combined in the brain of the dog.

The dog was presently thrilled by something so nonsensical as a bell.

This impact is referred to as conditioning. The first reaction evoked by the second stimulus (Food) is now evoked by the First Stimulation alone (Bell) in the idea that 2 stimuli zone units are constantly combined. This is without the U.S.A. knowing it all the time. Some items that we eat as a child with our parents are, for instance, the favorite meals for several people. The favorable emotions of being with the family and the particular meals in our brain have probably occurred. As a consequence, we tend to have at present the warm, lukewarm feeling that we get with family from the disbursement of our meals alone, even if our family is not present when we consume it.

Though you acquire a certain atmosphere, you can always respond in a way that allows you to use classical purchases to enhance your performance if you understand what you are doing, what Pavlov did you do precisely. You just connect dull stuff again and again (such as a ringing bell) with beneficial ideas and emotions. Very quickly, this boring stuff will mechanically produce value. This is the traditional purchase at the job. This can help you think you have these little beneficial times that maintain you energetical and reasonable as a consequence of once your region has been moving about, perhaps even feeling tumbled by pressures or difficulties.

6. Think good, but not too abundant, and once you should believe negative.

Naturally, positive thinking has its advantages. But positive thinking is not always the most efficient answer. Edges are sometimes also negative ideas.

If we tend to be dissatisfied or grieving in the region, having adverse ideas and displaying the feelings created by those thinking enables America to transmit to others that they tend to be supportive and kind. Our thoughts can inspire the US to act, change our lives, and change the planets if we're treated under the belt and become angry. If these negatives are casually pushed aside without serious consideration of their roots, these effects will be negative. Then question yourself; once you are specialized in the negative, does this adverse emotion lead to an intervention that will improve your lives? If so, then maintain it. If not, operate to modify it.

7. Practice Feeling

There is a unit AN of endless things about which to be upset, sad, or worried. But the reality is that there is also a range of items that make you feel passionate, happy, and enthusiastic. We must decide to specialize in this. It is up to us.

One way to train your brain to get a beneficial impression. Gratitude, for the people, stuff, and feelings, is once we tend to feel or special gratitude. If we tend to feel particular at the job, we tend to earn the consideration and friendship of those with whom we operate. If we tend to thank our associates or colleagues for our region, they are friendly and helpful to the United States. When we tend to thank the unit for the restricted stuff that is going on in our everyday life, we realize many of that in our life. Do you have to create a routine of sensation? Try to follow the sensation of these five directions.

8. Savor the Good Moments

Too often, without really celebrating, we tend to let the sensitive moment slip by. Perhaps you are given a small donation by your buddy or laugh by a partner. Do you pause to notice these little places that life should give and enjoy them? If not, you can take advantage of the taste.

Enjoyment merely implies that we hold on to our sensitive ideas and feelings. You can taste by sticking to the feelings at useful times. Or you can enjoy the beneficial experiences you have come home. Enjoyment is a great way to create a lasting stream of healthy ideas and feelings.

9. Creating good feelings by viewing fun videos

The expanding and constructing hypothesis indicate that favorable experiences build our psychological, mental, and social assets so that America can take advantage of much of our experiences. But do we tend to inject a small explosion of beneficial emotion into our life? One way is to view videos that are good or enjoyable. Cat clips or sacred videos create a quick increase of positive feelings that can help fuel beneficial feelings spiral upwards. Be good only to emotionally hold the beneficial feelings that arise by means of methods like saving, so that when you leave the sofa, you will take your sensitive atmosphere. And make sure that you don't get stuck too soon; otherwise, you may feel responsible for not getting much done.

10.   Stop Dwarfing your success

We have a foolish practice of diminishing our achievements and not fully appreciate our gains. We've always been successful. For example: "I didn't increase my happiness as much as I wished," or "anyone could use positive words." This, however, doesn't recognize how difficult you are simply putting in efforts not being placed by everyone. Instead of celebration, these words minimize your tiny achievements.

I'm fighting a bunch with this. People can commend Pine Tree State for constructing my own company, which enhances people's happiness and well-being. But I'm going to tell you, "Nobody can do it. This kind of thinking undermines all the little effort I make to make my company happy. Everybody was able to do this, but they haven't.

For you, the same applies. Even reading this article all the way up to now indicates that you are striving to increase the capacity to believe that you are good. Don't pay any cash to you. While you are good about your thoughts, joy, or well-being, take notice of your victories, whatever the purpose. Celebrate a little after every small victory.

If you read a situation as all sensitive or all dangerously, you can stop imagining all or nothing. This is yet another difficult adverse way of thinking. For instance, I may assume that I'm not good at being able to serve kids by fostering skills that make them think they're good and make them happier. I even had to close off my first company to nurture children's well-being.

On the other side, I have been very successful in working with companies in order to help them create their happiness applications, write material for these goods and classes, and sell workbooks for people to know how to be happy. What do you believe? What do you believe? Is this a mistake or a victory for the Pine Tree State? I would have to pick one or the other if I were previously prone to imagining all or nothing.

There is always plenty of room for improvement, but don't think you are a complete failure just because you don't really succeed in the way you have hoped for. You're winning, and you're losing. This is life. This is life.

Positive Thinking, Negative Thinking, Right Thinking

The beginning of your life's continuous and lasting change is to understand the distinction between positive thinking, adverse thinking, and "correct thinking." Consider the one who lives down to perform the piano. There is no harmony, no equilibrium, and no true tuning when he performs, as he always hits all the incorrect notes. Finally, the player is nourished by the disharmony and absence of fun and pleasure with his music and chooses to go to a conference center. Each one of the people has the authority to experience life with balance, equilibrium, and happiness, but we continue to want to understand the values and, therefore, the values. the teacher suggests, "You have the capacity to perform, but you want to understand musical things. Life operates by physical legislation and principle. If not, because there would be no gravity, no electricity, and one plus would not equal two, you couldn't fly the AN aviation.

The universe's rules are entirely confident.

Not only is universal law reliable, but it is also sculpted in stone.

You can count on that, and when it works. Essentially, you won't let the universe down. It does not matter how young, how thin, how fat, how fat, how slender, your faith, your nationality, or whether or not you join a male or female. The power, the power, and the energy are separate, and our ideas and views guide it.

Your Word is the Law

Your Word is the Law within the universe is your term. However, you want to comprehend this legislation. You can't generate what you want without AN's knowledge of laws through ignorance.

It is the law of cause and effect that is essential to all the distinct legislation. The law of cause and effect states that the outcome or outcome of any circumstances is the cause. The reason is always AN idea or conviction. The instance of sowing and harvesting, intervention, and response is another way to describe the laws of cause and effect.

Or placed into a contemporary context-my region of thoughts has developed my outcomes.

Like the sunlight, the law of cause and effect is impersonal. You obtain the heat and healing effects of the sun's rays if you stand in the sun. It seems that the sun doesn't shine on you if you're in the shade. But you were hit in the shadows by UN agency? Did you move into darkness in the United Nations agency? The reality is that as a consequence of our ignorance, we tend to unite darkly.

The Problem with Cognitive Content

I repeat, is impersonal in the law of cause and effect. That is why we see so many people that the most sensitive zone unit has so many problems and disasters in their life. This person misuses or misunderstands the law somewhere in his or her life. It's not that he or she's wrong. It doesn't mean that she or he isn't a fool. It implies that this individual misused the law through ignorance or incomprehension. This can be used for every building. For instance, aerodynamics or gravity will not kill you but, even though you are a sort of loving, positive person, a misunderstanding can.

The world is like a river. The stream continues to flow. It does not matter if your region unit is glad or disappointing, good, or bad; it just flows. Some individuals go down to the river and scream. Some people go down to the river, and the area is happy, but the waterways don't matter; they just flow. We are going to use it and make luxury, or we are going to dive in and die. As a consequence, the river merely flows unchanged. It's with the universe, therefore. The world in which we reside will either promote the United States or ruin the United States. It is our understanding and application of the legislation that determines our impact or outcome.

We shall obtain only what is acceptable to our minds.

We will take a teaspoon to the watercourse, and someone else may go with a cup. Another person can guide a bucket, and another can go with a barrel. However, there is an abundance of watercourses and waiting forever. Our conscience, thoughts, reference framework, and belief systems determine whether, or not, and we approach with a tea cubicle, a cup, a bucket, or a barrel to the watercourse of existence.

If we unit in our imagination is poor, and we're only able to curse our little teaspoon on the watercourse of existence. We may have many things to curse other UN agencies as we do. But remember, -anything that we tend to curse can kill the United States. There's the river, and abundance overflows. With a teaspoon, a box, or barrel, you will come back to the watercourse of life any time you like. The river of life is all the way to the United States. We have the only restriction. The truth, if we hand over the idea that we don't have it, we'll have something we want. It's just that easy.

Beliefs Become Limitations

All our experiences have resulted in the United States to think about stuff related to us. Whether or not this region of views is real is important because if it's real, it is real for the United

States. It becomes law in the universe if we speak our word long enough. Provide your limitations with sufficient vigor, and they are yours. Whether your belief is accurate or totally foolish, if you embrace it, that is your life.

Once we accept a thought, the moment has come, and nothing can prevent it. it's a concept whose time has come. It is a concept whose time for America has arrived if we have adopted a concept of absence and restriction. We will do nothing about it except to change our minds. It is preparing to develop when you plant a seed. You're going to have a tomato when you grow a tomato.

As it thinks a cucumber would be better for you, the tomato won't change its mind and become a cucumber. The soil will provide you with tomatoes, even if you are sensitive to tomatoes until you plant them.

Look at the convictions which shape the basis of your existence. We are packed with views, behaviors, ideas, opinions, and conditions that we have gathered over many years. We have my beliefs together, and you can wander around like this, and this is where I have been based all my life, so now you're an area unit which says that I might be wrong. I don't want to hear that. "So, we tend to live with a set of faiths called faith, s We know that when we are challenged, we dig in our heels, usually," I don't want to tell me anything fresh.

Many of the items we tend to think —gathered from past experience, people's organizations, and individuals—do not appear real, but they unite what we speculated should live out of.

Because we can live and want a robust unit in a certain region, we create laws concerning the essence of existence and how things develop, and these laws become convictions. These convictions, unfortunately, will also become restrictions.

We can only succeed to the extent to which we are a unit ready to cast away our wrong views. Break Through wrong convictions. It's because of the limitations in our own mind when we tend to know the disease, inability, or absence.

While we all understand that our lives do not work in boundary fields, the trick is that we are still scared of amendments. Our device is secured into our comfort zone, regardless of how suicidal it will be. However, it's only to be awkward to get out of our temperature and be free of our problems and constraints. We are only going to know freedom directly in ratio to the quantity of reality we tend to accept as a unit without operating methods.

We should stop taming, blaming people, and prevent unpleasant choices, and face the fact that we have tended to accept unworkable convictions that this region brings together the immediate cause of what is happening in our life. It's not about moving from the negative to the positive. It is a question of shifting to "correct thinking," which means working towards understanding the complete reality of the UN organization, our connection with life and unit tends to be a reality.

Right thought, based mainly on and not on illusion, is that the foundation determines the solidity of every other thought. The system of our belief filters positive thinking and negative thinking. Correct thinking is based on knowing the truth or the truth of any scenario.

Set Yourself Free with the Truth

You always get the facts about any situation you are worried about, by knowing the truth. Look behind your current faith and lift your Higher Self, "What is the reality about this?" If you can hear the reality, your Higher Self can forever reveal the reality. You are correct to think about victimization when you influence that reality. It's not about being positive or bad; it's just you. Every situation in the region in which you come together can settle completely if you allow your Higher Self to disclose the truth. This may sound magical, but only the law of cause leads to intervention.

The initial objective of success Since the beginning of your moment, the objective of all excellent lecturers has been to bring us to the truth that we strive to create our own reality. More importantly, we are responsible for all that occurs in our life. This includes excellent, bad, and hideous things.

If we believe that one thing or another is the cause of our problem, we will always be looking for the solution away from ourselves. To look for the responses to our issues, in reality, we first need to look at a fresh way, which can lead the United States to monitor individuals and activities in a different manner. The outside world is a replica of our inner world in many respects. You need to be aware of that. How many troubled individuals have you taken notice of this reality by the UN organization? No determination, no input, inspiration, or encouragement will fix our problems if we tend to search for the response.

Law of Attraction

All emerges to us through the main fundamental law of physics-LIKE ATTRACTS LIKE! The law of attraction is called this.

Mathematical accuracy is applied to the Law of Attraction, like all-natural laws. He's unbiased and impersonal, suggesting he works once you want him and once you don't want him.

It has nothing to do to be "nice," "bad," or anything else together with your character, cultural faiths. Beyond this Law, nobody lives. It's an undisputed law as true as the Gravitational Law.

No one realized it existed before the law of gravity was recognized, and yet it still influenced everyone. The Law of Attraction is like that. Most individuals know that it does not work mechanically, but still, everyone is littered with it.

But the law of gravity works not to stop you from moving into space. You need not understand the mechanics. You do not want to understand the mechanics, but in your lives, the law of attraction functions.

You may not have done it until now, but you are encouraged, drawn, and formed to everything you experience in your lives. No exceptions are made. That may not be great news if the way you want your life doesn't go. And since most of us do not appear to be too proud of what we have created in our lives, we have become extremely talented masters who draw an overflow of circumstances we do not want.

The mind draws anything, you know. Awe-inspiring experiences attract a fearful mind. A troubled mind creates more perplexity. The plentiful mind draws plenty.

Since we tend to capture what we wish to do, the subconscious thinking habits that govern our lives make sense. Positive thinking and positive thinking ultimately impact your lives positively by altering your manner of looking at difficulties and errors. The next section will focus on and significance of self-love.

Chapter 6

Loving Yourself

Pierre Corneille Self-love feels narcissistic in the ground; after all, who would only love himself would become in vain.' Self-love is the cause of every other enjoy.' But self-love varies from narcissism because it concerns self-respect and private well-being rather than a mere need to be careful and loved to cope with our own insecurities and questions about self-esteem. Self-love, which only saves your energy without any benefit, is crucial to combating anxiety, concern, and rethinking in adverse topics.

It is essential to have a fundamental knowledge of who you are in a group if you want to manage your lives. We are the key to our lives by our self-image, which our own image is the one we tend to keep in mind. This shaped picture is consistent with all of our deeds, emotions, or behavior, and even our skills. We are nearly the type of person we tend to think we are a unit. What we want to remember is that as soon as we keep this picture, no effort, determination, engagement, or self-command will lead to the United States being an alternative technique, because we are always inclined to use our own technique. To be different, we tend to look at our self-image first, however.

Our Mental Blueprint

From infancy, we gather many thoughts that we consider good or harmful, wise, or silly, confident, or frightening, and thus on. These often-fake identities weaken our self-image through repetition. Either the U.S.A. can be content and unsuccessful or tyrannized by this self-image. Whether or not we are inclined to realize it is a mental plan within ourselves. It's an image of the technique we think we tend to have a zone unit. This plan is accurate and finishes to the end. Our self-image is this overview or scheme. This plan isn't, however, who we have the inclination to zone unit. We tend to assume that we have a tendency to area unit. Our own image may have had entirely inaccurate or disproportionate circumstances or conditions, but they are uniformly accurate, as far as we are concerned. We do not question the legitimacy of this information when we record. We cannot even remember how or wherever we tend to obtain this information most often deliberately. We just live the way we did. We think that, even if it's not accurate.

The Secret of the Ages

The overwhelming number of people cannot understand the message that every excellent instructor has been trying to communicate with his fellow human beings since the beginning of recorded history. The secret, the most amazing reality that so few understands, is that you are spiritually full and ideal at the stage of your Being, which we will determine for your Higher Self.

Just as a sea fall has all the characteristics of the sea, so you have all the characteristics of the Creator in you.

Science, philosophy, and religion all teach in their own way that in the universe, we are one power and with the power, the energy, the force, or anything with which you are comfortable. In the end, we are one power. You and I are personalized representations of all the universe's power. You can call it your Higher Self.

We're not going to ruin the US Upper Self. We're going to deny that this is there, we're trying to hide and laze it, but we don't tend to change the reality, that we are a UN organization. What we want to do is to recognize that we have a tendency to district unit and to know how our ideas can be transmitted.

Who You Are is Not Similar to What You Are?

We should see that we are different from the United Nations organization; we have a commitment to the zone unit, and what we do. Whoever is spiritually good in our inclination towards the zone unit, but what we tend to do is not always outstanding. The difference between who we are and what we are inclined to do is created by ignorance. It follows that our activities will only be outstanding if we do not understand that we are tending to be a spiritually great group.

I want you to attempt and immediately do one thing. Tell yourself only. "I know that my spiritual excellence is the United Nations organization." Listen now in your head to your small voice. It is likely communication with your voice, "Oh, no, I'm not." It truly threatens to threaten your ego. Your ego sends you back immediately the question: "What do you mean you are ideal? Go home now, take a nice look, and look at how you treat others. Do you remember what you were doing last night? You constantly rumble. How about your mother's, father's, boss's, and cousin's treatment? You want to check yourself foully. You want to identify with all you are not. They want you to build up and feel guilty, along with your actions. You want to decide, reject, and blame yourself for not meeting your own and other photos and aspirations. You have to recognize that your ego tries to trick you. This doesn't really mean you.

Your Ego is Tricking You

It may be your own excellence to assert yourselves. It is not a journey of ego that asserts your perfection. It is an ego journey not to confirm your own perfection. Remember, your first and most important stage in your life is to understand that you are spiritually whole, full, and ideal, regardless of what you want, want to do, or have to do.

Neutralizing Your Ego

It's like you unreservedly, the way to neutralize your ego. You don't bloat your ego loving yourself. Actually, loving yourself neutralizes your ego because your ego doesn't worship you.

We want to understand that life is awareness. That means that for the US, what we suppose is true. We can experience whatever we are aware of. In fact, what we are profoundly confident of is what we can know in life. This is a significant declaration. Therefore, in existence, we experience what we are profoundly confident of. If our patterns of thought say, "I can't do that or that, I can't merit that or that, I'm a bad individual," we proceed to create circumstances in keeping with our conceptions of evil, absence, and restriction.

The bottom line is this: If we cannot agree to ourselves that we are dignified and worthy, we will not be able to settle for the worthy and worthy unit of this alternative folk region and will do so on their judgment.

The alternative is for us and others to grow their love. That's the only way we can always be safe. First and then others, we should be able to accept ourselves completely, realizing that everyone else is so, as we are spiritually outstanding.

You have Created Yourself

You have developed yourself, whether you realize it or not, in a significant manner. You borrowed, imitated, or created your own personality characteristics, mannerisms, forms of speech, facial expressions, gestures, and even methods of thinking and thinking. It could have been of an excessively large novel or a film by a parent or other parents, a favorite teacher, a friend, or an artist.

Perhaps you borrowed from someone you didn't want. Maybe it was from some UN organization that you felt uneasy or scared. It could have been some way to construct that individual to imitate you feel less frightened and discouraged.

Never Reject Yourselves in Any Way

You need to check the temperament you developed. Maybe because you were an associate imitator, you can find one of the reasons you can keep from doing so. It is not unusual to cause hunger. It can help to understand that no one is from scratch producing a Self. All have a comparable problem to do. Of what is out there, everyone decides. Even if you have imitated your temperament, you are not a fake. No one else has ever combined exactly the same as you did. Don't miss that there are twelve notes alone in the region, and yet several thousand distinctive and magnificent blending areas have been produced. All of it is a question of how you find your location.

It doesn't construct you to be a new individual taken from others. The great problem with this is that you can change it at any moment since you put it together from scratch. You never stuck. You are never stuck. It's not a catastrophe to discover that you're not the person you believed you were. It's the start of the catastrophe, on the contrary.

To change the experiences you experience, it is essential, to begin with, a transparent knowledge that you can never help yourself by dismissing a quarter of yourself. We get hated because we tend to create a picture, but we expect that our families, peer groups, companionship, religion, and the community where we live always have to take the foundation. The sad half could be that we cannot live up to the pictures, pictures, designs, norms, or ideas of how we are always inclined to assume that we must be. It's a dead-end for psychology.

Freedom Begins with Self-Acceptation

We permitted our ego to manipulate us into an insufficient, insufficient, uncertain, silly, poor, evil, or undignified method of cognition. All this can be described as bad inefficiency and bad self-image. We will still have bad self-esteem and a bad self-image until we construct a conscious call to change our thought habits. In your lives, the first and most important thing is to accept yourself, to enjoy who you yourself are. You can only start to like others once you are interested in yourself. Many people believe they must first state that they have to tell themselves and love others. Well, that method doesn't operate. The reality is that you first have to face all the errors-all, the presumed crimes that have been committed, every time you felt like a jerk, and the whole day you acted inadequately. You must be prepared to stand in front of the entire globe without an apology. If you do that, you come back from an unconditional love situation.

How you see yourself produces your conduct, creating your workplace or outcomes. This behavior You determine dissatisfaction when you link your self-worth to your achievements and/or conduct. No matter how difficult you attempt, someone will believe you're not all right. Remember this: in somebody's sight, and you could always be a failure.

You won't all over, not even a majority sometimes. Consider how much your existence is about obtaining approval and understand that needed reality: you might not receive the approval you are seeking! You just can't help everyone, therefore learn to please yourself, and you're a UN organization.

You Can't Fail as An Individual

It's worthwhile continuing that the UN organization in your region is spiritually outstanding, but it's not always outstanding what you do. What you do may be successful or failing, but by the fundamental mental method, you will be detached from the outcomes and will never be a success or inability to support what you have and do. There is no way you will only fail as a person in existence. That's not how you came about.

You're in suffering when you hate yourself for all that you did or did not, or when you hate other people for what they haven't given you. Suffering is a form of self-determination. It's a way to get irritated. It is disappointing for you not to live up to expectations that we are inclined to have something about ourselves or that someone else has people if you really get to know that anger and pain and an absence of happiness in our lives are right there.

I have discovered that the main reason for their conduct is self-hatred while collaborating with people from United Nations agencies. Their self-hatred was the reality that they had not met the standards of someone else. Most of us decide to think of what we have or don't have and what we did or what we didn't have.

We think we've let others down once we tend to unite a mistake in the region.

We do not say that we are not intelligent if we tend not to live up to our people's expectations, employers, religion, family, or partner. This is called the judgment of oneself.

If you judge yourself, you are going to decide that you are wrong. And once you're placing yourself for one thing you did, or something that wasn't accomplished, or a position wherever you're foiling someone else, you feel bad. But the only way to sculpt the very small lack of judgment is to sculpt it. It's not going to be nice; it's just destruction.

It is true that everyone in the U.S. has stuff in our life that we tend to regret, but we tend to avoid moving and regretting houses for some reason.

The class must be found, and the skill is thrown away.

So long we tend to area unit against each other, we won't be for anyone. Being against others means being against us. This is a psychological and spiritual truth. The most corrupt thing we can do is judge someone. One of the main adverse and self-destructive behavior a person can have is to remove another person and remove the life of another.

Release with Yourself Everyone What if you had no regrets from the past? Try to figure out what would occur when, whatever they did with you, you completely forgave everyone in your life? Hoped you would make sure that you preserve unhappiness, poverty, illness, lack, and limitation in your life in the way that you cannot excuse, be it yourselves or anybody else.

Many people don't want other people to apologize. You tell stuff like: "Why when they came to me, should I let them go off the hook? The enemy always is someone we imagine that is going to harm America or take away something from us, but it is not true that anyone is going to harm America.

Through ourselves, people harm the US. They don't actually harm the U.S.A. to the least. However, we give instructions for treating the United States, and they obey it.

Call instantly to ransom you, as you will eventually be destroyed in the end. "Yes," you say, "I agree with you, but you don't recognize my circumstances, you really hurt Maine. Maybe I'm going to give up the rancor at some point, but right now, I can't give up." Understand that this mentality is dangerous and dangerous to you more than it is to the individuals whom you are feeling. "The pupils and followers replied." It was an exemplary life you lived. You brought the U.S.A. out from the Moses area. He softly answered, "When I met my Maker, he will not lift:' You were like Moses and Salomon? You judged us demonstrating wisdom like Salomon. "It's going to wonder,' Were you yourself? The tale demonstrates that people lived to be their own throughout time. Why do we still have a desire to fight?

It's because we have to help others that fight.

You're sure that you will be angry with somebody-your boss, wife, relatives, and kids by assuming your own destiny. At first, it will be a solo technique to assume your own destiny, and it can seem that everybody is against you. But your own picture is the only one you have to stick to. The views of those who agree or disagree with the region are irrelevant.

Your own obligation is the choice to assess your lives. You are responsible for the results of your own lives. Your own accountability is your decision or your inaction. Alternative people can often have values and convictions that clash with you. And when you see yourself living against their principles and convictions, it can be appalling because, in some manner, it is threatening their basis.

When you face your faith, the inner fight of nursing is waged by an Associate, and the fight is, "Could they potentially be correct? And if they are, then I can be incorrect." The UN organization knows who they are, is not susceptible because of people's views. Those who are insecure in their region and do not understand the United Nations organization can always be scared by any UN organization which threatens their own scheme of faith, directly or indirectly.

How Are You Doing It?

Does anybody like you, let me lift you? Are you confident? Do you hold commitments you only make for yourself? You're a good individual, does one guess? You lock your region most of the moment, or did you develop an undertaking to cowl yourself up to the department of the United Nations? If you're treating a UN agency lover, you're treating yourself or talking to you the ways you believe you see yourself, breaking commitments to yourself, do you think you're going to maintain him friendly? Facing it, probably you're not going to need such an individual.

It is very important to look at the technique we tend to handle ourselves.

We unite our own most serious foe most of the moment. We have a tendency to think that we might not like what we see. We are united fearful of meeting our inner selves.

I often hear people say, "I want a little more to discover myself, but I'm scared what I'm trying to solve with regard to myself. I'm scared of the strange creatures I can notice on the trip or the process." Understand this; obviously, there is no reason for the reality of yourselves to be frightening.

Self-worth is Self-worth. This is why it is not known as "Other worth."

You will no longer be in a situation to love yourself if your value derives from others. If you are an infirmary partner, you are an infirmary partner in everyone else. An aware individual is self-aware. He understands his own nature, so he understands all about the same nature of the other UN agencies. Know yourself as a unit in the region, and other people as it is.

Never worry about exposing yourself to vulnerability. It's the start of force to expose a weakness. Keep in mind-all you learn is nice news. It's always great news, regardless of how troubling or amazing it may be. Keep this in mind, particularly in times when a fresh reality strikes with a conviction that you only have to give up, but that a region unit is unwilling to do so. In return for a diamond, a wise individual is prepared to give up a little coal. Have the bravery to do so, and you start to change yourself.

You should not have other people's approval to change your life. Don't question, "Is this right to visit against all that I was instructed to think?" Say instead, "Let me see, however, much strength that I can put in my quest." Your own wish for private liberty is that the only search warrant that you each wish.

If you will learn a little about the reality of yourself and live your life, as you are capable of living, a lot of people do not like that because they are not engaged in the same path as you are. Will you deny yourself wealth because of other bad areas? You'll deny yourself the safety of the zone unit because millions of people are ill? Take a good look at what you deny and never believe in yourself as "false" for having what you want.

We are supposed to make errors while on the route of finding. You are not the so-called errors, defects, sins, or mistakes. Make sure you are apart from what you have and what you do from the United Nations agency. As you come to realize that everything that is happening in your lives is transient and can always be vibrant, you transcend what is happening in life. You need to understand that your Higher Self is unmodified. You believe that what you have and what you are doing is the true you when you create your transitional nature. Perhaps the greatest mistake you're going to make in your lives.

You need to separate from what you have and what you are doing from who you are to encounter your own magnificence. Learn how to separate the performance of your performer from the performer but not to participate in what happens in your life.

When you sit on the sea and look at the ship's sailing around, there is no issue as ##t as you stand and look at them.

You only experience pain and suffering once you create yourself with the vessels.

If you say, "That's my ship," then once it passes out, you're going to be grieved. You will sleep in fear of someone else becoming its leader if your state,' I must control that boat.' We also prevent our damaging association with our temporary mistakes, defects, and mistakes by simply watching and perceiving our errors and unfeasible conduct while not judging it.

You come to the stage wherever you begin to recognize that all power is within you, as you begin to honestly challenge and appear during adulthood. We search for alternative agencies to educate the United States of what we should do, but only we can always realize what we are trying to do.

Did you ever wonder why the unit of folks conned by artists is sure? It is not possible to have an artist with someone UN organization. It is difficult for people to understand why others benefit from it. The reason why you get used is that you give away your power, and you don't have to answer for your own life. You don't have to choose your own, so you allow others to attempt and do it for you. But understand this reality: they're going to do it TO you if you allow others to attempt and do it FOR you. As soon as you allow others to be responsible for your lives, they will manage your fate.

Why Would You Like Your World to Differ?

We can note that other regional units have responsibility for this, but we have a tendency to limit our freedoms by this kind of thinking. It's simple to say.

Again, to make our thinking more straightforward is to separate what we have from and what we tend to do from the UN agency, the "doer" is to be separated from the "deed." The mystery of this globe must be measured, but the universe must not live in us. Our ship is needed inside the sea, but on our ship, we tend not to need water. We start sinking when the water is on our ship, and we should ransom as insane as if we were floating. The issue is that we frequently realize that we are drowning in our lifetime's water of physical impacts.

After we drown, because we traumatize the others, we do not acknowledge others except to combat them and attempt to change the conditions.

May I lift you before I go any further: "Why must you change your universe?" Each moment we tend to plan to change whatever is happening around us, be it company, work, government, family, partner, or whatever, we are under the illusion that these groups of individuals and activities do one thing for America.

In fact, our intention is to differ in relevance to our knowledge.

People and events don't do anything to the United States. They just trigger feelings that already exist in the United States. If we return to the fundamental concept of life, we realize that in the globe, nothing takes place that we do not allow deep in our conscience. There are many forms you think it is accomplished to you, and sometimes the region of belief unites terribly deeply. Everything in our core is aligned primarily with our external experiences, although we may not be consciously aware of them. I understand it is difficult to simply recognize stuff that you do not need deliberately as a consequence of a unit of areas in your lives.

The reality of the issue is, however, that you're satisfied with something deep within.

Just imagine a sad person in the house saying, "I'm going to change my life." He's just as sad as before then. He decorates many times, and in himself, he still doesn't feel any shift. Know you those who think that they can dynamically modify their happiness levels? Did they develop an error wherever? Where are they going to make their own corrections?

You will learn what is really happening if you are frank with yourself and examine what is occurring in your lives in the right way.

Therefore, if we are inclined to try and make sure that unfailing areas change the exterior results, we will only produce the same expertise once more. However, internal features don't change.

This self-assessment method is a great way to find yourself if you do not understand what to attempt and do anymore. It will help you to know that the process of mechanical thought cannot climb up to its own limited stage.

Do not try to get rid of fear if you are unsure what to do or if you have any anxiety. Keep wherever you go, and let it say something exceptional to you, and it will.

The reality about you, therefore, is that you're not what you get and what you're not what you do. You are fully and perfect spiritually; your achievement and happiness in existence are proportionate to the capacity you have to acknowledge this reality.

Auto-esteem versus narcissism We, as a culture, have an incredibly strong influence on the value of shallowness and, therefore, the dangers of narcissism. And that's something good. However, how we feel about ourselves determines that we tend to deal with people in the United States and vice versa. In 1890, William James recognized shallowness as a basic human being, not less vital for survival than feelings like rage and fear. And yet, we do not generally live the different differences between insufficiency and self-importance, or our behavior and responses do not consider us to support the contrary as aggressive.

Terrorist theorist Dr. Sheldon Solomon says that shallowness is "contentious because some people argue that it is essential for psychological and cultural well-being, whereas others argue that shallowness is irrelevant or linked with magnified abuse and cultural failure." Self-esteem varies from narcism by representing a nursing partner intended to realize achievements we have, values to which we have adhered, and care for others. Conversely, narcissism frequently reveals a fear for success or weakness, a focus on oneself, a healthy drive towards finest perception, and an inherent sense of insecurity and insufficiency. So, from where do they come back? And why are we inclined to write them?

"Vanity is an imaginative self-image, created once people replaced vain praise, and a fake accumulation of $64000 in affection and recognition they did not need for their children," says our fresh novel, The Self-Under-Beating. "Vanity is an imaginative self-image, a creation of which people have made up when people replace blank love and fake love and recognition." On the other side, parents United Nations Agency units are adapted to their young people and are really sensitive to them. These kids develop up with the right UN agency's nursing associate and good shallowness.

Studies have shown that children have offered compliments for skills they have not gained or have skills they don't have, as if they had got no longer in the least, often emptier, and less safe. Only young people commended for their true achievements have been able to construct inferiority. The others had something much less desirable to create— narcissism. Unnatural stress or unsuccessful accumulation leads to increased insecurity and anxieties, which promote narcissism against security.

Narcissism promotes jealousy and aggressive rivalry, which promotes empathy and collaboration. Narcissism promotes domination, where shallowness recognizes equality. Narcissism means stupidity, in which stupidity represents humility. Narcissistic critique is offended, where feedback increases shallowness. Narcissism necessitates pulling others down so that they are placed on top of them. Self-esteem causes each person to be perceived as a significant person in an extremely significant universe.

The society contributes to the promotion of self-esteem or narcism. Dr. Solomon describes that "self-esteem is eventually a cultural structure because the value norms by which people decide to respect social norms in the region." These norms can either give methods of people feeling intelligent or can support fantasy expectations, which will only ruin their insignificance. Solomon remarks that a guy in America needs to be wealthy and unsuccessful, and a female needs to be "young and thin as a little pulp, and that's not feasible." He said: "Our children's region, tutored at an earlier era, must adhere to a set of principles that are not realistic to the typical person. They found that a strong and possibly successful defense against existential anxieties, which is intrinsic in our human condition, was the sense that we are inclined to a region unit eve. In fact, they revealed that the reason why, as James stated, "self-esteem is a basic human desire, indispensable to our survival."

You can navigate your lives in a manner you want to know, significance, and value by feeling nice about yourself as an individual, appropriate to the United Nations organization. In order to reach a manner, we should recognize ourselves as a value-for-minded member of a community that is one thing. Ernest Beker stated, "the seemingly old-hat terms ' self-esteem' is a measure of the terrible nucleus of human adaptation. To give and offer the key to the realization of our value, compassion, help, and empathy. If we tend to recognize that our time on earth is fleeting, we will be satisfied with the painful fact which each intervention has extra power, every moment. It also provides America a good opportunity to benefit from the moment we have, and therefore the people we tend to share it. Therefore, constructing self-esteem is a feeling of belonging, friendship, and equal treatment between our fellow human beings on the far side.

Are you very particular? No other individual like you is there. You deserve to be loved not just by your fellow men but by the leading character in your lives— YOURSELF. Practicing self-love will be difficult for a lot of people, particularly in moments when we tend to encounter severe difficulties. It's not a matter of being self-interested or self-loving, but of getting our well-being and happiness in a little bit with ourselves. We use self-love, so we tend to break through our limited convictions and lead a truly shining existence.

So, take the favor, take a profound breath, grab a very little hug, and start engaging as follows

1. Start with one very beneficial thing every day. How well you have done things, how lovely you now look. Whatever can make you smile.
2. Fill your body and make it flourish with meat and drink.
3. Move your beautiful flesh every day and learn to enjoy the skin in which you live. You can't hate your way into being affectionate.
4. Don't believe everything you think. Don't believe everything you think. In America, there is an interior critic who tries to keep America small and secure. The downside is that America jointly finishes living a lifetime.
5. Encourage and encourage individuals from the United Nations organization. Just remind them that you are superb but just superb.

6. Stop comparison. Stop comparison. There's nobody on this planet like you, so you can't compare yourself with someone else. The only individual with whom you have to compare is you.

7. Finish all interactions with nephrotoxicity. Seriously. - Seriously. Anyone who makes you feel superb needs to be no part of your lives.

8. Celebrate your victories regardless of how large or small. Pat on the back and be pleased with what you have accomplished.

9. Step away from your comfort zone and see something fresh. It's unbelievable that when we have a tendency to, we realize we have achieved one thing we didn't understand or suppose that we could do before.

10. Use the stuff you make differently and enjoy them. That's what you're all about.

11. Be aware that beauty can't be described. That's what you think. Let no one of these magazines from Photoshopped make you want your body not to be perfect. Even in the real world, these models do not look the same.

12. Take your ##ja every day to relax. Breathe in and out, clear your thinking and be.

13. Follow your love. Follow your love. You understand that problem, which excites you, but at an equal moment, it frightens you. However, you have to attempt to convince

yourself that this is not going to work. You ought to go and do it!

14. Patient but continuous. Self-love is always changing. This is something that you want to do daily, but it takes a lifetime to learn. So, help yourself and be kind in the exhausting moments.

15. Be aware of your thoughts, feelings, and desires. Live your life in respects that reflect it.

16. Give love and regard to others. It allows us to feel greater when we are inclined to treat others as we are willing to expect to be treated. This doesn't mean that everyone can always repay their favor, but that isn't their disadvantage.

17. Look for one thing every day to be thankful for. It's unavoidable you plan to spend your days. It's beautiful and very human. These days it is particularly important to look for at least one problem for which you are thankful because it helps to move your mind and power around what is happening.

18. Reach family, friends, healers, and anyone you need to help you through the mighty moments. You shouldn't pass alone through them.

19. Learn to say no. Learn to say no. Typically, saying no doesn't make you a fool, it makes you a sensitive individual.

20.   Forgive yourself. Forgive yourself. Do you understand that you likely only once (or possibly occasionally) felt hazardous, embarrassed, disgraced? It's time to let go of it. You can't change things that have wiped the past, but your future is managed. See it as an experience of teaching and think that you can differ.

21. Just write it down. Write it down. Swim with so many ideas that a headache gives you? Write down everything on a piece of document, no matter how insane, medium, sad, or frightening it measures. Keep it in a diary, break it up, fire it up, and attempt to let it go, whatever you want.

22. Switch on and off. Take your favorite tea, coffee, and wine with you, no matter what you choose, and just sit on your own for a few minutes. No television or entertainment, only you think of the fantastic things, which are taking place without delay in your life, what the measure of your big dreams is and how you will build them.

23. Give up the need for other parties ' permission. — Dita Von Teese 24: "You can be the ripest, the most judgmental fish in the globe, and there is still somebody who loves peaches by the United Nations organization. Be meaningful. Be realistic. Every single moment of each day on this planet, nobody is pleased. You understand why? You understand why? As a consequence, we tend to

evaluate all human beings squarely. We make errors, we feel (nice and bad) feelings, and that is all right

24. Give yourself humanity.

25. Make yourself creative and categorical regardless of strategy. Painting, writing, sculpting, building, music, whatever takes your fancy, and make positive you permit your inner critic at the door. There are no right ways to be inventive.

26. Let the trauma and injuries of the past go. This can be highly strong, and one of those moments you would like to help others. The reality is, however, that it is almost a kind of weight that is elevated from our shoulders when we tend to give up stuff happening to America. With America, we don't have to perform that anymore. We're more elevated.

27. Find a happy location. Find a happy location. Where are you comfortable, calm, pleased, good, and up to date in life? Go to this location when you rummage about adversity or think about yourself. Think of how it works, of how it tastes, of how it appears.

28. The next moment you are pleased, create your finest characteristics and achievements on top of the planet. It may sound a platitudinous touch, but it is a fine reminder when every day you measure it is superb.

29.Contact your internal conversation. It is time to create a modification if it is not affectionate, helpful, and helpful. You deserve to talk to your comfort, sibling, brother, daughter, or child within the same strategy.

Thirty. Have fun! Have fun, have fun! Go forth and do the stuff your heart is lighting up. Discover them, appreciate yourself, and appreciate your incredible lives. Self-love gives you eventually the positivity to fight depression, fear, concern, and rethinking.

Chapter 7

You Can Do It!

"Believe in yourself, and the rest will fall into place. Have faith in your own abilities, work hard, and there is nothing you cannot accomplish" - **Brad Henry**

Everything you need to overcome overthinking and its underlying mental conditions such as depression, anxiety, and worry are already inside of you. Live according to your own terms, follow your heart since it already knows the right direction to go accept yourself regardless of your flaws.

How to Follow Your Heart

But in spite of life attempting to pull you in a very million directions, there are ways that you will carve out a sacred house for yourself. You can do your best to measure consistent with your heart's want, which can assist you in getting pleasure from the life you reside and be a lot of gifts to the individuals around you.

Part 1: Identifying Your Heart's Want

Make a list of belongings you wish to accomplish. A "bucket list" can facilitate you fathom that direction your heart desires to travel in. Try to set goals that you just are probably to be ready to accomplish (not "be the primary human on Mars"). This list can be an excellent supply of inspiration once you are checking out significant events to figure toward in your life. If it's truly from the heart, it will replicate a number of your deepest interests and aspirations. Create an associate open house. The first step to going in together with your heart this means is to allow your heart the time and house to talk up. It's important to take a seat still while not distractions for your heart to be ready to let itself be detected. You may wish to form associate intentional place wherever you'll visit simply sit. If you have an additional room in your house, you can lightweight some candles and build a snug atmosphere for this task.

Listen to your heart. Once you've set the right conditions, you can begin to try and do the work of being advertently receptive to your heart. You may wish to raise yourself an issue, such as "what am I feeling under the surface right now?" Wait a short time once you raise the question to examine if a response bubbles up from your heart. This kind of practice can facilitate your heart and your inner desire, express itself.

You can additionally use a method referred to as Focusing, which is nice for obtaining in a bit together with your body. Here's how to do Focusing:

Once you've cleared the house and asked what is going on within you, pay attention to what your body answers with. Don't attempt to explore it; just notice it from a distance. For instance, you may feel a tightness in your chest once you raise what is going on beneath the surface. Notice it from a distance.

Put a handle on the sensation. This is usually within the kind of a word or short phrase. For instance, you can say "tightness" or "chest pressure" or "tension." Keep trying words out till it looks to work the feeling. Go back and forth between the feeling and also the word that describes it. Check and see how they move. See if the body sensation changes a little bit once you have the correct associate name for it.

Ask yourself what is inflicting this sensation. What is it about your life without delay that is inflicting you to feel tight in your chest? do not grasp for a solution, just let the response bubble up. This may not happen the primary time. Focusing can take observe, but this is an excellent series of steps to assist you in opening yourself to your heart and everything that is happening within you.

Set aside time day after day. A hectic life will extremely dampen your ability to follow your heart. Take time out of your day, every day, for yourself. Don't let something else impose on this point. What you do with it's up to you, but here are a few suggestions:

Meditate. There is a range of mental and physical health advantages to meditating, such as lower pressure and lower stress. Try sitting upright for at least ten minutes in a very quiet place. Focus on one thing, such as the feeling of air getting into and out of your nostrils, or an object like a pencil. When your attention leaves the object, gently remind yourself to come back. Take a long bath. Relaxing in water has similar effects to alternative relaxation techniques. It's a good way to wind down. You can use this point to replicate on your life, or just get pleasure from the silence and sensation of a heat tub.

Have a coffee date with a friend. You may not get to pay the maximum amount of time catching up with friends as you'd like. Use this "you time" to invite a cherished friend to own lunch or coffee with you.

Find interests that activate your heart. Society places a big stress on the brain. It says that you should "think before you act" and keep rational decisions. However, this doesn't leave a lot of area for your intuition or your heart. These things can build life pleasurable instead of routine and economical. Finding activities that touch your heart will facilitate keep the pathway open, rather than only partaking the planet together with your brain.

For instance, if you like to read, make positive to permit time for reading in your schedule. Ask your friends for recommendations for smartbooks. A poetry collection will be particularly redolent.

If you're a lot of a moving picture buff, check out some highly rated films that may tug on your heartstrings.

Spending time in nature is another smart option; it will facilitate you feel a lot of alive and connected with yourself.

Part 2: Organizing Your Life

Seek medical care if it looks useful. If the problems obstruction you from following your heart appears a lot of serious than you'll upset on your own, or with help from a friend, consider seeing a healer. Many therapists deal with this sort of downside on a daily basis. If you had a traumatic childhood, a bad wedding, or if you've simply folded beneath a ton of stress, therapy will facilitate you discover your heart and feel a lot of alive.

Somatic experiencing medical care is similar to Focusing, where you focus on sensations in your body instead of thoughts and recollections. Cognitive-behavioral therapy will facilitate you examine mounted thoughts and beliefs, which will be preventing you from following your heart.

Ask friends to facilitate. Sometimes it's onerous to break through to wherever your heart is all on your own. Enlist the help of a lover for this task. You can truly do Focusing with a lover, where you go through the steps along and report what happens. You can additionally simply bring up what is going on in your life without delay, and specific you want to urge a lot of connected together with your heart. See if she has any advice for you. Talking it out can additionally facilitate because expressing your emotions in words has a powerful result.

For example, you can say, "Hey, I feel like I'm not extremely following my heart in my life without delay. I could extremely use somebody to speak to regarding this. Would you be willing to help?"

Live your own life. It's easy to measure our lives in response to pressure from others, such as friends, family, a spouse, or even kids. If you want to follow your heart, make positive you're living consistent with your own needs instead of what others wish from you. This is actually one amongst the foremost usually reportable regrets from folks that are on their deathbeds.

Ask yourself, "Is this what I truly wish, or am I doing it for someone else in spite of myself?"

There's nothing wrong with being generous and doing things for alternative individuals, of course, but you have got to seek out a balance wherever you're faithful yourself once you are being kind and serving to others. Otherwise, however, smart your intentions, you can simply give way and lose your affiliation to your heart.

Commit yourself to your path. Changing your mind will be a straightforward answer to adverse things, but if you perpetually back out, you'll ne'er learn from your mistakes or build any progress. It's important to decide on the trail you are on in life. Commitment will offer you the strength to hold on within the face of the issue. Following your heart isn't perpetually presupposed to be simple. If you feel a lot of resistance toward this sort of commitment, whether it's to education or an explicit career, then it might be an honest plan to look at whether or not you are extremely following your heart.

Avoid mistaking natural resistance and issue with this kind of bigger resistance. It's normal to feel pessimistic typically, even if you're on the correct path for you. If you aren't positive if you are doing the correct factor, try asking somebody you trust, such as a detailed friend or friend.

Clean and organize your personal space. You might be stunned by what quantity your atmosphere affects your mood. Color, for instance, can have a massive result on however individuals feel. Make positive your house is clean and well organized. Paint the walls a different color if you do not like them. Decorate with a design that evokes you and provokes a "beauty response." Have pictures of your darling ones around. Doing these simple home organization techniques can include modification; however, you feel and build it easier to access your true want. Clutter and a poor atmosphere will cause litter in your mind, which can limit your ability to follow your heart.

Part 3: Acting on Your Desire

Engage in communicatory activities. There is a range of inventive activities you'll do to urge connected together with your heart. The goal here is to open yourself to your heart or your innermost desire. Styles of style, like those employed in art medical care, will assist you in becoming a lot more receptive to yourself and your heart. Here are a few ideas for belongings you will do:

Music - Try connection a choir or taking stringed instrument lessons.

Art - Take a painting class or learn, however, to sculpt.

Dance - Enroll in a condiment category or maybe exercise-dancing categories at the athletic facility.

Drama - See if there are any open theater teams around you that you will be a part of. Acting is a good way to precise your creativity.

Free-Write - Life can cause your true needs and your daily routines to get crusty over with obligations and expectations. A practice like free writing will facilitate you access your heart and start to develop a more in-depth relationship with this essential part of yourself.

Choose a topic and write it at the highest of a chunk of paper. The topic will be one word, like "travel," or it can be a brief statement, like "what I think regarding traveling." Set a timer for 5 or ten minutes and take a look at to jot down regarding the subject while not putting a lot of thought into what you are doing. Don't set up ahead of time. The goal is to let your unconscious mind take over for you instead of letting the center a part of your brain holds the reins.

Practice Attentiveness - There are 2 totally different ways that you'll live your life: being and doing. The "doing" mode is what many individuals notice themselves stuck in a very ton of the time. It's a necessary mode for our fast-paced, high-stress culture, and it's actually terribly helpful for keeping up. However, the "doing" mode can build it onerous to listen to your wants and curtail enough to get pleasure from life.

Mindfulness meditation will facilitate you strengthen the "being" mode of your life, which is the mode that may assist you to begin to follow your heart.

Sit in a comfortable, upright position. Get used to this position for a number of minutes. Begin to pay attention to what is going on in your experience. You will have a lot of stray thoughts, body sensations, and seemingly random emotional surges. Pay attention to all or any of those things and the rest that happens, doing your best to require a "curious" stance toward them, where you do not get to react to them. Pretend you are someone and you would like to watch this expertise while not intervening. Once you've done this in a safe, quiet, sitting environment, you can attempt it in your way of life, whereas you are doing alternative things.

Make a Massive Move - Based on your bucket list and overall life goals, decide to make an enormous move if necessary. This could be going back to high school for a lot of education, moving to another city with higher opportunities or family within sight, or quitting your job to do something that resonates a lot of closely together with your heart's want. It may be an honest plan to speak to your friends and family regarding the move before you begin shifting gears, to see what they think and enlist their support.

Make Little Changes - You don't essentially need to build massive changes to alter your life and start to follow your heart. See if there are very little things you will waste your daily routine to feel a lot of attuned to yourself, and you want. For instance, you may wish to pay longer together with your friends or spend less time in front of the TV. Consult your bucket list to see if there are minor changes; you'll build on your life so as to attain what you actually wish out of it.

Understand That Perfection is Fool's Gold

Name one person you know the World Health Organization is flawless by all standards and definitions. (Don't say, God. God is not a person)

A simple google search provides the subsequent definition of the word perfect: "having all the required or fascinating parts, qualities or characteristics." The word "desirable" is the key to know our futile obsession with perfection. Desires are never-ending. As soon as one wants is happy, a new one comes knocking at the door. Perfection or flawlessness is the desired state.

And the interesting factor is, it always remains the desired state. It never becomes a reality. Here is an example: Tom, who makes $20,000 a year, thinks "my financial scenario would be good if I build $50,000 a year". Fast forward five years and Tom is currently creating $50,000 a year. That's his perfect money scenario. Yet currently, Tom feels "my money scenario would be good if I was creating $100,000 a year". The definition of his "perfect financial situation" changes once he gets there.

We will solely pursue perfection and perfection. We will ne'er deliver the goods it as a result of it doesn't extremely exist. It is just like the carrot tied ahead of the donkey and also the donkey eternally chasing it. It can never reach the carrot as a result of once the donkey moves, and the carrot moves with it. We are like the donkey, and, the state of perfection is that the carrot.

Understanding the Nature of Flaws

We were created with flaws. We all have some gaps in ourselves that we have a tendency to attempt to fill throughout our lives. This is the thrust of existence — the journey from being this to becoming that. Stephen Hawkings, the great uranologist puts it in perspective: "One of the basic rules of the universe is that nothing is ideal. Perfection simply doesn't exist.... Without the state, neither you nor I would exist" —Stephen Hawking.

We are not turning into better when we have a tendency to are an effort to alter by mending our flaws. Rather, we are simply dynamical in our state of existence from being this to being that. This process of becoming or evolving or changing is life. Life is a journey from being flawed to becoming perfect. Imperfection to perfection. This continuous process of becoming is the cloth of all existence. Everything is evolving, changing, becoming one thing alternative than what it's — every moment. You are no exception to that.

Don't Take the Game Too Seriously

Flaws are OK. Flaws are smart. We exist because of our flaws. Don't you see, that's the entire game. This chase for perfection or flawlessness is our life force. The problem starts once we take this game too seriously. We become all serious and tense up in our pursuit of removing all our "flaws."

Is it wrong to try and take away my flaws? Is it wrong to attempt for perfection? No. There is nothing wrong with needing to remove your flaws. It goes wrong when you become too finite and high regarding this game. When you forget that in the end, this is just a game, a play. It goes wrong when you start hating your flaws with a burning passion. When your flaws build, you grit your teeth and clench your fists. The answer is to first all settle for your flaws. Don't be bitter. Once you do that, life is no longer a struggle. It ceases to be a struggle and becomes fun. From flaw to flawless. One flaw at a time. Enjoy the game.

"Flaw" Is Just a thought. A "flaw" is just an idea. In reality, there is no such thing as a flaw. Blindness is not a flaw in a very country of blind individuals. You are 5ft8inches tall. You want to be 6ft tall. So, your height is a flaw consistent with you. For someone World Health Organization is 5ft3inches tall, your height is perfect. It is not a flaw for that person.

Your flaw is someone else's perfection. Here is another powerful idea: "Your flaws exist only in the lightweight of the existence of others."

If you were the only living human within the world, you would not have any concept of flaws in yourself. Nobody to compare yourself with. Hence no flaws.

Everything Is Perfect because it Is

You have two selections. You can settle for your flaws, and change them, playing on and enjoying the journey. Or you can cry and complain regarding it all you would like. When you settle for your flaws as a district of you, they cease to be flawed. They are there; however, they don't hassle you any longer.

Accepting yourself doesn't mean acceptive solely the smart and positive aspects. It means acceptive your flaws and negative aspects too. Aside regarding yourself becomes a "flaw" once you prefer to see it united. And that choice can greatly impact; however, you read yourself. Accepting your flaws can enable you to settle for yourself absolutely. And that will empower you on the far side of your wildest dreams. Self-acceptance is power.

Say a certain quality in yourself that you see as a flaw, is bothering you too much, then raise yourself this question: am I able to do one thing to alter it? If affirmative, then go ahead and alter it. If no, then learn to accept it wholeheartedly as a district of yourself. What's more? Once you learn to accept your own flaws, you become more acceptive of others and their flaws too. You become less judgmental. And that sets you free on numerous levels. You become more relaxed. Less rigid. Slowly, you come to the realization that there are not any flaws, no mistakes in existence. Everything in existence is ideal, even when it doesn't seem that way.

So, at the end of the day, your flaws don't even matter. Stop losing sleep over your so-called flaws. Accept yourself as you are and permit yourself to feel powerful. Set yourself free from these limiting notions of being flawed or imperfect. They do you no good. And they waste some time and energy. Just perceive this: "There are no mistakes existing. Everything is perfect because it is." At the end of the day, you are the best person for yourself; no one else is as aware of your needs and wants as yourself.

Conclusion

In this book, overthinking and its underlying related mental conditions, including anxiety, worry, depression, and fear, are explored with focus placed its beneficial role in our lives. Armed with an understanding of the root components of overthinking, the reader is made aware of when overthinking becomes a problem. The serious consequences of overthinking are specially made clear to the reader, so they can identify it when it shows up, especially its paralyzing and delayed effect on decision making. Next, the causes and solutions to overthinking and its underlying mental conditions are covered, which include changing one's perspective, socializing with loved ones, engaging in relaxation techniques, therapy, self-love, and acceptance.

Psychology concepts such as the law of attraction and self are also explored in this section of the book. After that, there is an emphasizes on the importance of positivity and positive thinking to shift one's mindset away from a negative and self-destructive one. The book ends with an encouraging message that urges the viewer to be themselves and go with their heart in life.

Overall, this book is an exploration of human psychology, especially our insecurities, anxieties, and stresses, as well as a guide to solving it. It hits close to home because it tackles mental health conditions that many of us struggle with and attempts to make some sense of it in the modern world. Ultimately, in order to overcome overthinking and its underlying mental conditions, one must be willing to change themselves and reach out to others, most importantly. Self-improvement is something that requires mentors and support in order to accomplish; else, a person feels isolated, giving them no reasons to leave their minds and become a part of society.

* * * * *

www.ingramcontent.com/pod-product-compliance
Lightning Source LLC
Chambersburg PA
CBHW061804250726
48657CB00001B/276